EXCEL

A Quick Reference of More Than 300 Microsoft Excel Tasks, Terms and Tricks

2002
FROM A TO Z

Stephen L. Nelson

Excel 2002 From A to Z:
A Quick Reference of More Than 300 Microsoft Excel Tasks, Terms and Tricks

Copyright © 2001 Stephen L. Nelson

All rights reserved. No part of this book may be reproduced in any form or by any method or any means without the prior written permission of the publisher.

Published by
Redmond Technology Press
8581 154th Avenue NE
Redmond, WA 98052
www.redtechpress.com

Library of Congress Catalog Card No: applied for

ISBN 1-931150-22-2

Printed and bound in the United States of America.

9 8 7 6 5 4 3 2 1

Distributed by
Independent Publishers Group
814 N. Franklin St.
Chicago, IL 60610
www.ipgbook.com

Product and company names mentioned herein may be the trademarks of their respective owners.

In the preparation of this book, both the author and the publisher have made every effort to provide current, correct, and comprehensible information. Nevertheless, inadvertent errors can occur and software and the principles and regulations concerning business often change. Furthermore, the application and impact of principles, rules, and laws can vary widely from case to case because of the unique facts involved. For these reasons, the author and publisher specifically disclaim any liability or loss that is incurred as a consequence of the use and application, directly or indirectly, of any information presented in this book. If legal or other expert assistance is needed, the services of a professional should be sought.

Designer: Minh-Tam S. Le
Editor: Fred Lanigan

INTRODUCTION

You should find *Excel 2002 From A to Z* easy to use. You only need to know that the book organizes its information—key tasks and important terms—alphabetically in order to use the book. You'll find it helpful, however, if you understand what this book assumes about your computer skills, what you should know about the Excel program from the very start, and what editorial conventions this book uses. This short introduction provides this information.

What You Should Know About Windows

You don't need to be computer expert to use either this book or Microsoft Excel. Definitely not. But you want to be comfortable working with your computer and Microsoft Windows.

For example, you should know how to turn your computer on and off, how to start and stop programs, how to choose menu commands, and how to work with dialog boxes. This book, for the most part, doesn't provide this Windows information.

If you need this Windows information, you need to take the Windows online tutorial, get a friend to give you a quick tutorial, or acquire another book on Windows.

> **TIP** *Any short book on Windows will tell you what you need to know, but if you're a business user of Windows 2000 or Windows XP, you may want to look at the* Effective Executive's Guide to Windows 2000 *or the* Effective Executive's Guide to Windows XP. *These books supply a tutorial on Windows geared for business professionals.*

What You Should Know About Excel

You don't need to know anything about Excel to use this book. But because understanding the Excel program window will make using Excel and this book easier, let me identify some of the more important parts of the window (see Figure 1).

Introduction

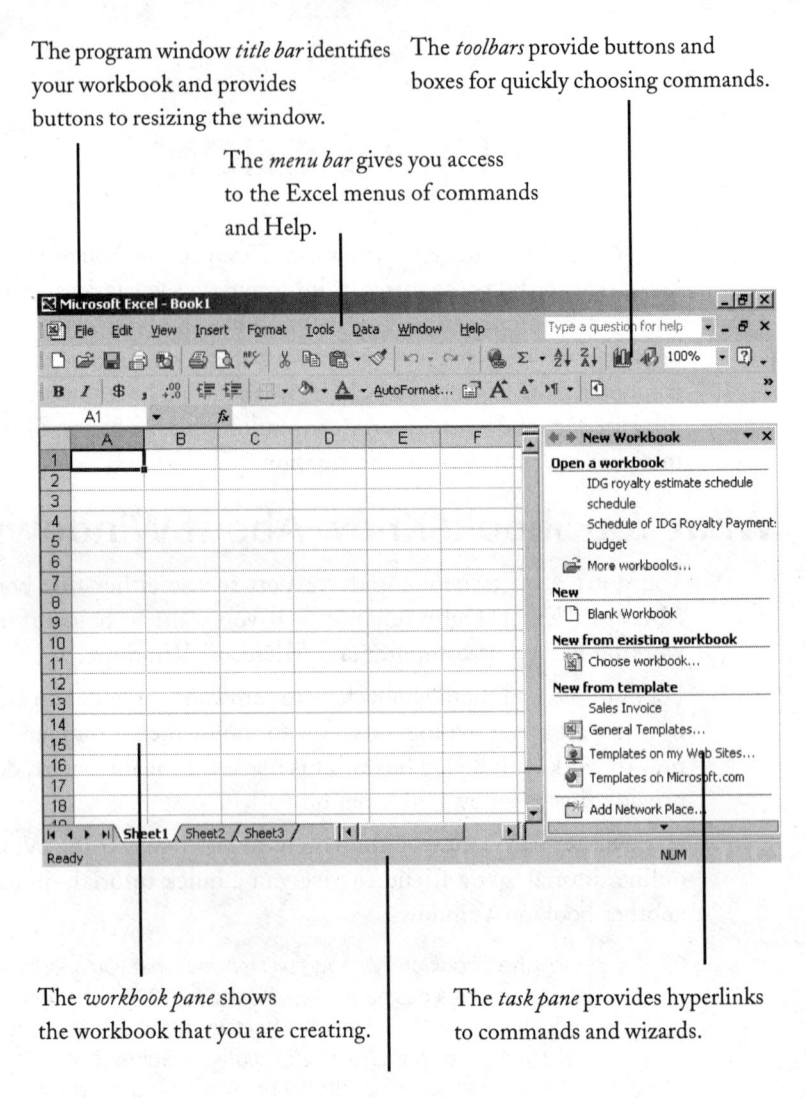

The program window *title bar* identifies your workbook and provides buttons to resizing the window.

The *toolbars* provide buttons and boxes for quickly choosing commands.

The *menu bar* gives you access to the Excel menus of commands and Help.

The *workbook pane* shows the workbook that you are creating.

The *task pane* provides hyperlinks to commands and wizards.

The *status bar* provides information about your workbook and what Excel is doing.

Figure 1 The Excel program window.

Let me also point out two important items about the Excel toolbars:

iv

Introduction

- Excel's toolbars vary greatly in their appearance. What you see on your computer will surely differ from the figures shown in this book. Excel personalizes your toolbars so that the buttons and boxes available are those you are most likely to use. Usually, you want personalized toolbars. If you don't, refer to the Personalized Menus and Toolbars entry for information on how to turn off personalization.
- While toolbar buttons and boxes aren't labeled, if you point to a tool, Excel displays the tool name in a popup box called a screen tip, or in earlier versions of Excel, a tool tip. This means that if you don't know which button is the Bold button, for example, you can point to buttons to see their names and learn their identities.

One other piece of information usually helps people just starting to use Excel. And here it is: Many of the dialog boxes that you use to tell Excel to perform some command include a preview area. This preview area shows how your settings look and therefore lets you experiment.

In the pages that follow, for example, you learn that the Format→Cell command provides a Font tab, which lets you change the font used for the selected text (see Figure 2). The Font tab includes a preview area that shows how your font settings look. The preview area helps you see the effect of your command specifications. Pay attention to the preview areas and you'll find that you can answer many of your own questions.

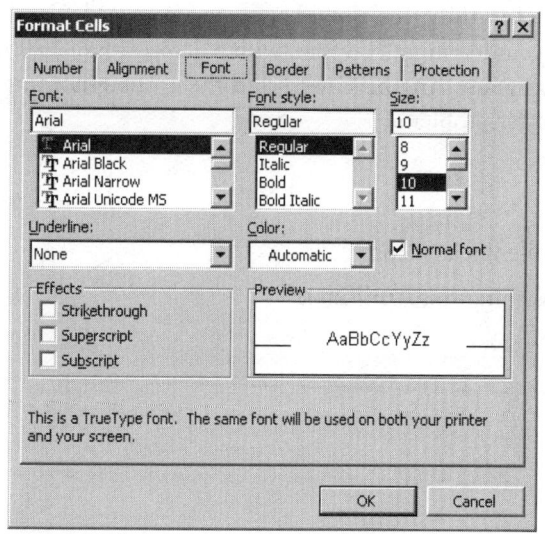

Figure 2   The Font tab of the Format Cells dialog box.

v

Introduction

What You Should Know About This Book

You already know the most important feature of this book—that it organizes its task descriptions and term definitions alphabetically. But let me comment quickly on the book's other conventions.

- The book doesn't include an index. That seems funny. How can a computer book omit an index? Well, the list of A to Z entries *is* an index. It's an index with information. I should also say that by omitting the largely redundant index, this quick reference provides an even longer list of task descriptions and term definitions.

- When this book refers to some box or button label, the label description appears in all initial capital letters. So, while the Font tab of the Format Cells dialog box includes a checkbox labeled "Normal font," this book would refer to the Normal Font box. The initial capital letters, then, signal you that the book refers to an onscreen label.

- This book's pictures of windows and dialog boxes may look a bit funny to you because they use a low display resolution to make the buttons, boxes and text look larger. Less information fits on the screen when the resolution is low, unfortunately, but what you see you can read. If the book's screen pictures had used a higher resolution, images would be very difficult to see clearly.

And that's everything you should know to get started. Good luck. Be patient in your learning. Have fun with Microsoft Excel 2002. It's an amazing program. And be sure to read the Troubleshooting entry if you encounter problems.

Stephen L. Nelson
steve@stephenlnelson.com
Seattle, Washington, April 2001

EXCEL FROM A TO Z

Absolute Cell References see Copying Formulas

Active Cell

The active cell is the cell marked with the cell selector (see Figure A-1). If you type something and press Enter, Excel places what you type in the active cell.

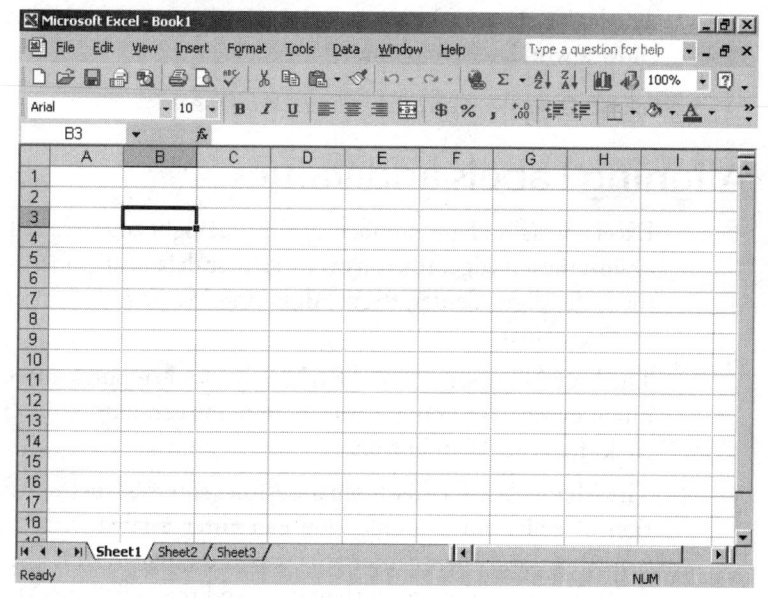

Figure A-1   The cell selector in cell B3.

SEE ALSO *Cell Selector*

Active Workbook

The active workbook is the workbook shown in the active document window. A workbook is made up of worksheets and chart sheets.

SEE ALSO *Charts, Macros, Worksheets*

Active document window

The active document window shows the Excel workbook you're currently working on. If you tell Excel to print, for example, Excel prints the workbook shown in the active document window. If you enter text by typing on the keyboard, Excel enters what you type into the active document window.

Excel adds a button to the taskbar for each open workbook. You can switch to another workbook, thereby making that workbook's document window active, by clicking the workbook's taskbar button.

Active Sheet

The active sheet is the sheet you see in the active document. It may show a worksheet or a chart.

SEE ALSO *Active Workbook, Charts, Worksheet*

Aligning Labels and Values

Excel normally aligns numbers against the right edge of a cell and text against the left edge. You can override these default alignments by using the Left Align, Center, Right Align, and Merge And Center buttons on the toolbar.

The Left Align, Center, and Right Align toolbar buttons work as you might expect. For example, to left align the contents of selected cells, click the Left Align button.

The Merge And Center toolbar button centers a label across a selection of cells. For example, you can enter a label in cell A1 of a worksheet and then center it across the range A1:D1 (see Figure A-2). To do so, first select the range, and then click the Merge And Center toolbar button.

Excel 2002 From A to Z

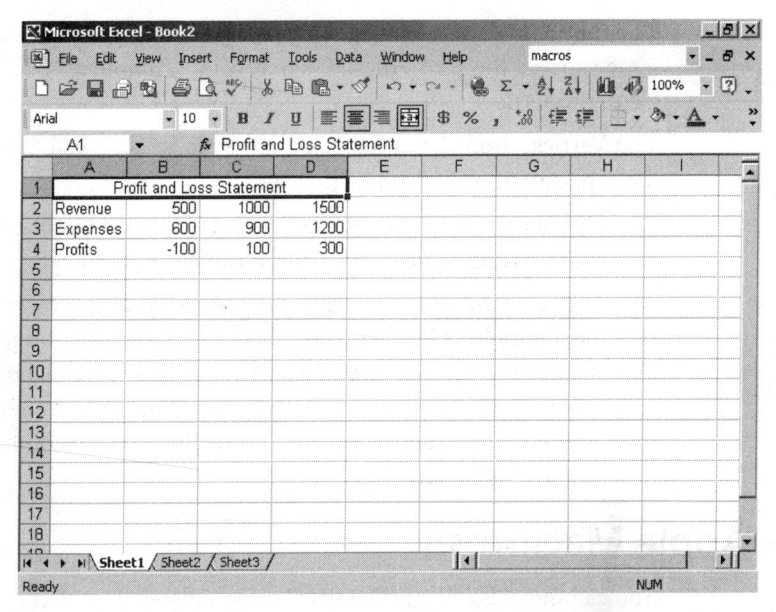

Figure A-2 A label centered across the range A1:D1.

You can access a more sophisticated array of alignment features by selecting the cell or range you want to align, choosing the Format→Cells command, and clicking the Alignment tab (see Figure A-3).

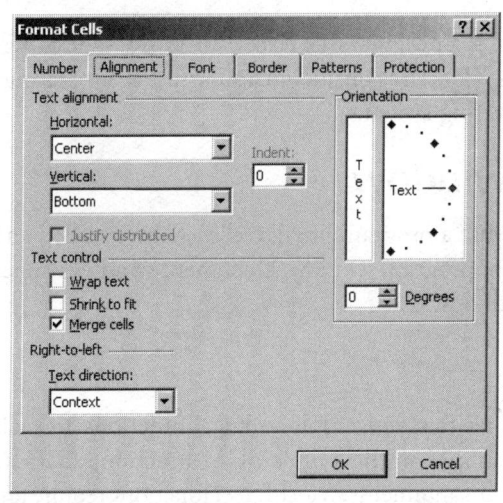

Figure A-3 The Alignment tab of the Format Cells dialog box.

3

The Horizontal drop-down list box lets you align cell contents in the same ways as the Left Align, Center, Right Align, and Merge And Center tools do.

The Vertical drop-down list box allows you to align cell contents at the top, center, or bottom of the cell.

The Orientation boxes allow you to rotate the cell contents either by clicking or dragging or by entering a value into the degrees box.

The Text Control boxes provide you with several more specialized alignment options. The Wrap Text check box allows you to split a long line of text onto multiple lines. The Shrink To Fit check box allows you to decrease the size of the numbers or letters in a cell so that they fit in the cell. The Merge Cells check box allows you to combine cells into larger, single cells.

Apple Macintosh

You can move Excel workbooks from Windows computers to Apple Macintosh computers and vice versa. Excel will open Excel workbooks created on either computer.

SEE ALSO *Workbooks*

Application

An application is a program like Excel. Or Word. Operating systems like Windows XP aren't considered applications. Operating systems are, well, operating systems.

Application window

The window that a program like Excel displays is called an application window, or program window. Document windows appear inside application windows.

Arguments

The input values that you supply to Excel functions are called arguments. For example, in the simple SUM function, =SUM(2,2), the values 2 and 2 are arguments. Most Excel functions require arguments.

SEE ALSO *Functions*

Array Formulas

An array is a set of numbers, such as 1, 2, 3 or 4, 5, 6. Array formulas use and return arrays. For example, if you add the array 1, 2, 3 to the array 4, 5, 6, you get a new array 5, 7, 9.

Array 1:	1	2	3
Array 2:	4	5	6
Total Array:	5	7	9

Array formulas let you use one formula to calculate an array of values. For example, if you entered the array 1, 2, 3 into the range A1:C1 and the array 4, 5, 6 into the range A2:C2, you can enter the array formula {=A1:C1+A2:C2} into the range A3:C3 to sum the arrays and return an array (see Figure A-4).

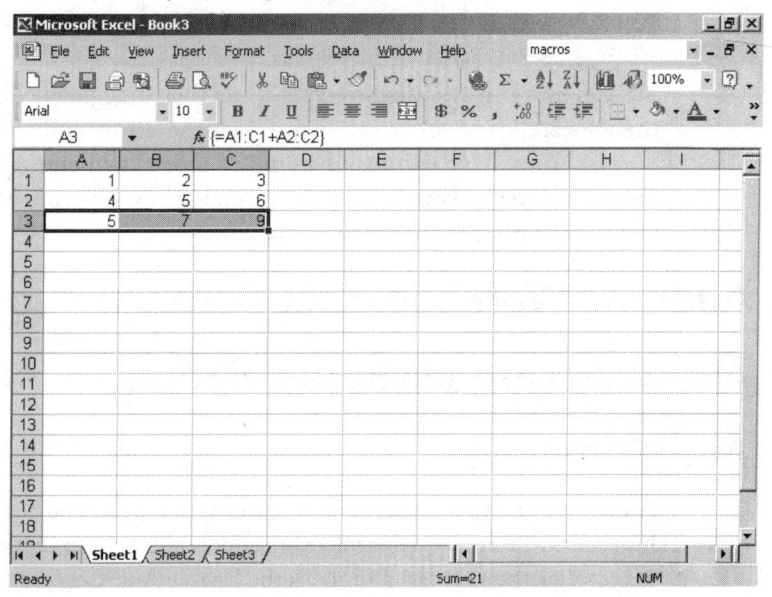

Figure A-4   A worksheet that sums two arrays.

When entering an array formula, you don't type the { and } braces. Excel enters these for you when you press Ctrl+Shift+Enter to tell it you want an array formula. To enter the array formula shown in Figure A-4, for example, you take these steps:

1. Select the range A3:C3.
2. Type the equals symbol, select the range A1:C1, type the plus symbol, and select the range A2:C2.
3. Press Ctrl+Shift+Enter to tell Excel you want an array formula entered into the range A3:C3.

SEE ALSO *Formulas*

Arrows

You can add arrows to your workbooks. Arrows are drawing objects. To add an arrow, first display the Drawing toolbar by choosing the View→Toolbar→Drawing command. Next, click the Arrow button on the Drawing toolbar. Then click at the point where you want the arrow to start and drag the mouse to the point where you want the arrow to end.

You can move an arrow by selecting it and then dragging it. To change the appearance of an arrow, right-click the arrow and choose the Format AutoShape command from the shortcuts menu. When use Excel displays the Format AutoShape dialog box, experiment with its boxes until you get the arrow you want.

Auditing Workbooks see Formula Auditing

AutoCalculate see Recalculation

AutoComplete

AutoComplete finishes recognizable words or phrases you begin typing into cells. To turn AutoComplete on, choose the Tools→Options command, click the Edit tab, and check the Enable AutoComplete For Cell values box.

Excel automatically completes labels you've already entered into the same column. You don't have to do anything special to use AutoComplete once it's turned on. If Excel guesses you're typing a recognized word or phrase, it completes the word or phrase. To accept the suggested word or phrase, press Enter. To reject the word or phrase, simply keep typing.

AutoCorrect

AutoCorrect fixes common typing mistakes. Excel already knows about many of the typing mistakes that people commonly make. For example, Excel knows how to correctly capitalize the first letter of a sentence and how to spell commonly misspelled words.

You don't need to do anything special to use AutoCorrect. Excel's corrections of your spelling and typing mistakes will occur automatically. (Try typing the word "and" as "adn" to see how AutoCorrect works.)

If you want to change the way that AutoCorrect works, choose the Tools→AutoCorrect command. When Excel displays the AutoCorrect dialog box, use it to describe how AutoCorrect should operate (see Figure A-5).

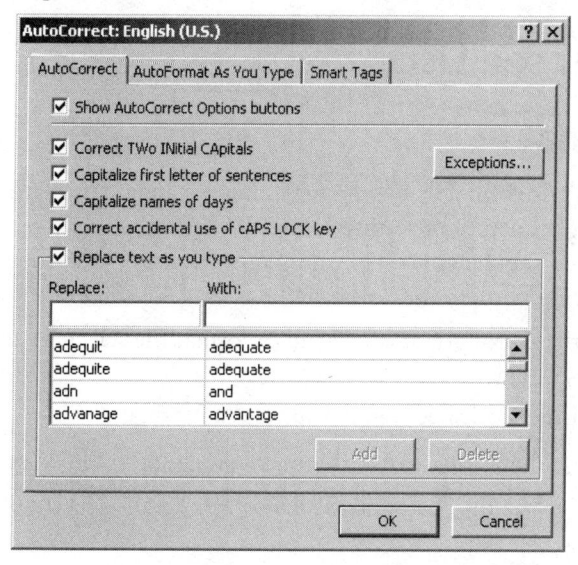

Figure A-5 The AutoCorrect dialog box.

You can uncheck the first box to tell Excel that you don't want the AutoCorrect Options button displayed after autocorrection occurs. (The AutoCorrect Options button lets you undo or adjust the correction.)

You can check and uncheck the next four check boxes listed to specify whether Excel should or shouldn't fix common capitalization errors. (Usually you want Excel to make such fixes.)

You can use the Replace Text As You Type check box to turn on and off automatic spelling correction and typo correction. (The list of corrections Excel will make shows in the list box at the bottom of the dialog box.)

To add a new common error to AutoCorrect's list, enter the erroneous entry in the Replace box and the correct entry in the With box.

AutoFill

You can tell Excel to continue, or *autofill*, a pattern of values in the selected range in two ways: You can drag the fill handle, and you can choose the Edit→Fill→Series command. The fill handle is the small square that appears in the lower right corner of a range selection.

SEE ALSO *Filling Cells*

AutoFilter see Lists

AutoFormat

Excel's AutoFormat feature performs many standard formatting tasks in a single operation: setting fonts, aligning labels, setting column width and row height, establishing numeric and date/time formats, and adding borders and rules.

To use the AutoFormat command to format the selected range, follow these steps:

1. Select the worksheet range you want to format.

2. Choose the Format→AutoFormat command.

Excel displays the AutoFormat dialog box (see Figure A-6).

Excel 2002 From A to Z

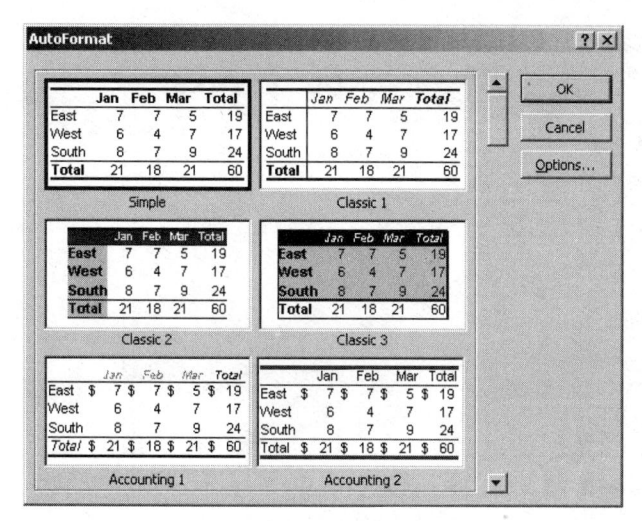

Figure A-6 The AutoFormat dialog box.

3. Click the Options button to specify which AutoFormatting options should be applied to your worksheet selection. When you do this, Excel adds Options check boxes to the AutoFormat dialog box. Select and clear these check boxes to selectively apply individual components of an AutoFormat.

4. Select an AutoFormat by clicking it. The AutoFormat pictures show roughly what the AutoFormat formatting looks like.

5. Click OK to apply the format to the range you selected.

SEE ALSO *Formatting Cells*

Automatic File Saves

Excel regularly saves a copy of the workbook you're working on just in case your computer or Excel crashes. It's this saved workbook that Excel opens the next time you start Excel after the crash.

To specify how often Excel should automatically save this copy of your workbook, choose the Tools→Options command and click the Save tab. Check the Save AutoRecover Info Every box and then specify how often Excel should save the copy (see Figure A-7). By default, Excel saves the AutoRecover copy every ten minutes.

A — Excel 2002 From A to Z

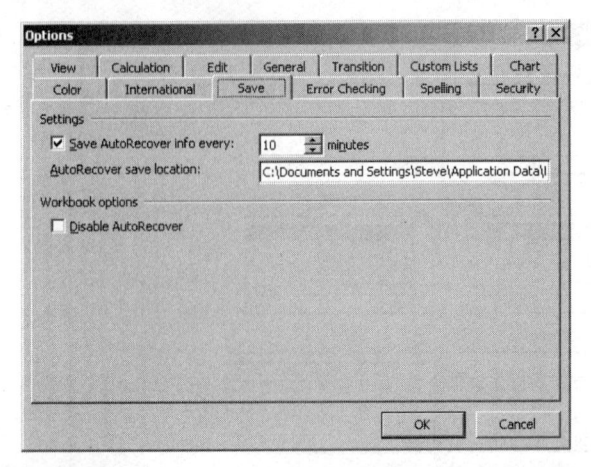

Figure A-7   The Save tab of the Options dialog box.

AutoRecover see Automatic File Saves

AutoSum

Excel provides an AutoSum button on the Standard toolbar that you can use to sum a range of values (see Figure A-8). To use the AutoSum button, select range that includes all the values you want to sum and one extra empty cell for Excel to place the =SUM function in.

Figure A-8   A worksheet with values that can be added using AutoSum.

In Figure A-8, for example, to add a SUM function to B7 that adds the values in column B, select B2:B7 and then click the AutoSum button. Excel places the formula =SUM(B2:B6) in cell B7.

Boolean Algebra

Boolean algebra tests logical conditions to see if the tested condition is true or false. For example, Boolean algebra can test whether 2+2 equals 4 and whether the value in cell B4 of the worksheet is less than the value in cell B3. If a Boolean algebraic test condition is true, the formula result equals 1, the logical value for true. If the test condition is false, the formula result equals 0, the logical value for false.

Boolean algebra expressions and formulas use the logical operators shown in the table that follows:

SYMBOL	DESCRIPTION
=	Equals
>	Greater than
>=	Greater than or equal to
<	Less than
<=	Less than or equal to
<>	Not equal to

Here are some example Boolean algebra formulas with descriptions:

FORMULA	DESCRIPTION
=(2+2)=4	Tests to see that 2+2 equals 4, returning 1 because 2+2 equals 4.
=(2+2)>4	Tests to see that 2+2 is greater than 4, returning 0 because 2+2 is not greater than 4.
=(2+2)>=4	Tests to see that 2+2 is either greater than or equal to 4, returning 1 because 2+2 does equal 4.
=(2+2)<4	Tests to see that 2+2 is less than 4, returning 0 because 2+2 is not less than 4.
=(2+2)<=4	Tests to see that 2+2 is less than 4 or equal to 4, returning 1 because 2+2 does equal 4.
=(2+2)<>4	Tests to see that 2+2 doesn't equal 4, returning 0 because 2+2 doesn't *not equal* 4.

> **NOTE** If you enter a Boolean algebra expression into a cell, you need to start the expression with an equals sign because the expression is a formula. However, you can also use Boolean expressions in logical functions such as the IF() function. In this case, you don't need to include the equals sign.

> **NOTE** Boolean operators have a lower precedence than the standard arithmetic operators.

Borders see Formatting Cells

Breaks see Page Breaks

Calculating Formulas see Recalculation

Cell Addresses

Excel uniquely identifies the cells in a workbook with cell addresses which you can use in formulas:

To refer to a cell in the active worksheet, you use the cell's column letter and row number. For example, to refer the cell at the intersection of column B and row 8 use the cell reference *B8*.

To refer to a cell in another worksheet, you precede the cell address with the sheet name and the exclamation point. For example, to refer to cell B8 in the worksheet named Sheet1, you can use the cell reference *sheet1!B8*.

To refer to a cell in another workbook, you precede the cell address and sheet name information with the workbook filename in single quotes. For example, to refer to cell Sheet1!B8 in the workbook named budget.xls, you can use the cell reference =*'budget.xls'sheet1!B8*.

> **TIP** The easiest way to refer to cells in another worksheet or workbook is to click on the cell as you're building the formula. For example, to enter the cell reference ='budget.xls'sheet1!B8 you could type the entire reference. Or, you could type the equals sign to let Excel know you were beginning a formula and then you could click on cell B8 in sheet1 of the budget.xls workbook and press Enter. Excel would then enter the cell reference for you.

SEE ALSO *Cells, Copying, Formulas*

Cell Borders see Borders

Cell Notes see Comments

Cell References see Cell Addresses

Cells

The intersection of a column and row creates a cell. Each cell has an address, or reference, consisting of the column letter and row number. For example, the cell in the top left corner of the worksheet is cell A1.

You can enter labels, values, and formulas into cells by clicking the cell, typing what you want to enter, and then pressing Enter.

SEE ALSO *Copying Cell Contents, Editing Cell Contents, Erasing Cell Contents, Filling Cells, Formatting Toolbar, Formulas, Labels, Moving Cell Contents, Values*

Cell Selector

A dark outline called the cell selector identifies the active cell. The reference of the active cell also appears on the left side of the formula bar in the Name box. If you type a number and press Enter, Excel places the number in the active cell.

SEE ALSO *Active Cell*

Charts

Excel's Chart Wizard lets you create charts using workbook data.

Understanding Excel Chart Terminology

Excel's Chart Wizard and documentation use several charting terms you'll want to understand as you begin using the Chart Wizard:

- The individual numeric values you plot in a chart are called *data points*.
- *Data series* collect related data points. Most charts you create will use more than one data series. For example, a chart might show both a revenue data series and a profit data series.

- *Data categories* order and organize the data points in a data series and are commonly based on time, such as months or quarters or years.
- *Data markers* are the graphical elements used to represent individual data point values in a chart. A chart that uses columns or bars, for example, has column or bar data markers. A pie chart has pie-slice data markers, and so on. Typically, the data markers in a data series all resemble each other.
- Excel typically describes and qualifies data markers using the *data-marker descriptions* such as axis scales and data labels. Different types of charts use different data-marker descriptions. Bar, column, and line charts use axis scales.
- A *legend* identifies the data series you've plotted.
- *Chart text* describes a chart or some part of a chart, providing chart titles, subtitles, and annotations.
- The *plot area* of a chart includes the data markers and data-marker descriptions.
- The *chart area* includes plot area, any chart text, and the legend.

NOTE   Excel limits the number of data points and data series you can plot in a chart. A data series may hold no more than 4000 data points. A chart may show no more than 255 data series. These constraints mean that you may sometimes need to arrange large data series or big sets of data series vertically by putting data series into columns rather than rows.

Using the Chart Wizard

To use the Chart Wizard, first enter your to-be-charted data in an Excel worksheet. Include not only the data series data points but also the labels that identify the data series and the data categories (see Figure C-1). Then, take the following steps:

	A	B	C	D	E
1		Year 1	Year 2	Year 3	
2	Revenue	500	1000	1500	
3	Expenses	600	900	1200	
4					
5					

Figure C-1   A simple worksheet with data you might plot in a chart.

1. Select the worksheet range that includes the data series and any data series names and data categories names.
2. Start the Chart Wizard by clicking the Chart Wizard button on the toolbar or by choosing the InsertÞChart command. Excel displays the first Chart Wizard dialog box (see Figure C-2).

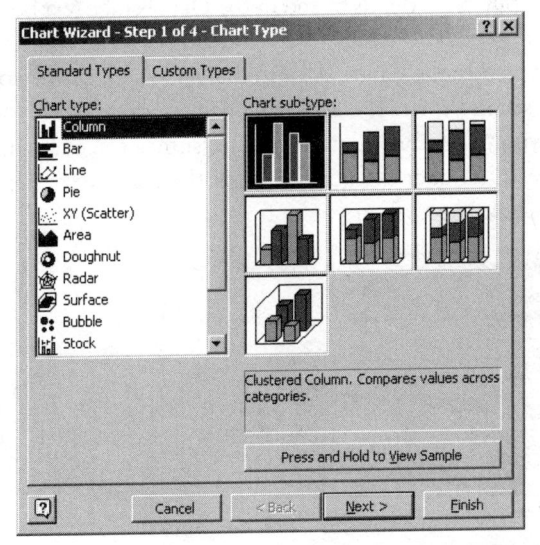

Figure C-2   The first Chart Wizard dialog box.

3. Select one of Excel's chart types from the Chart Type list box. Excel provides 14 different types of charts: Column, Bar, Line, Pie, XY (Scatter), Area, Doughnut, Radar, Surface, Bubble, Stock, Cylinder, Cone, and Pyramid.

NOTE   *You can return to a previous Chart Wizard dialog box by clicking the Back button.*

4. After you select the Chart type, Excel displays the different versions available for the chart type as clickable buttons in the Chart Sub-Type box. Excel displays a short description of the selected chart sub-type in the area below the Chart Sub-Type box. To select a chart, click the button that looks like the chart you want. After making your selection, click Next.

NOTE   *You can tell Excel to display a rough-draft version of the chart you're creating by clicking the Press And Hold To View Sample button.*

5. When Excel displays the second Chart Wizard dialog box, use it to verify that Excel is retrieving the correct data from the worksheet (this should be the case if you select the data correctly in step 1) and that it has correctly identified the data series (see Figure C-3). If Excel hasn't correctly interpreted the to-be-plotted data, click the worksheet button at the right end of the Data Range text box. When Excel minimizes the Chart Wizard dialog box, select the correct range. To restore the Chart Wizard dialog box, click the worksheet button a second time. If Excel has misinterpreted how you've organized your worksheet data—Excel assumes the chart has fewer data series than data categories—click the other Series In option button. Click Next when you're finished.

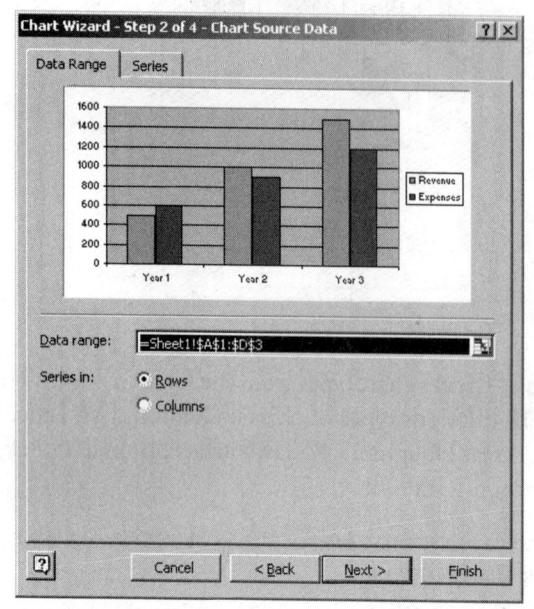

Figure C-3   The second Chart Wizard dialog box.

6. When Excel displays the third Chart Wizard dialog box, you use its Titles tab to add a chart title and axes titles (see Figure C-4). To add such chart text, just click the appropriate text box and type the text you want. Click Next when you're finished.

Excel 2002 From A to Z

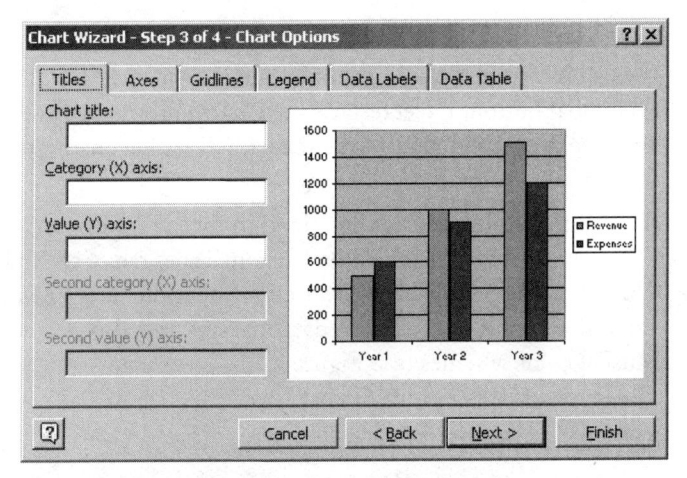

Figure C-4 The third Chart Wizard dialog box.

> **NOTE** *Excel updates the chart picture shown on the third Chart Wizard dialog box for any text you add.*

7. Use the fourth Chart Wizard dialog box to choose which location you want for your chart (see Figure C-5). To add the chart to a new sheet, click the As New Sheet option button and then enter a name for the new chart sheet. To add the chart as a free-floating object to an existing worksheet, click the As Object In option button and then select the worksheet from the As Object In drop-down list box. When you complete this step, you've finished creating the chart. Click Finish.

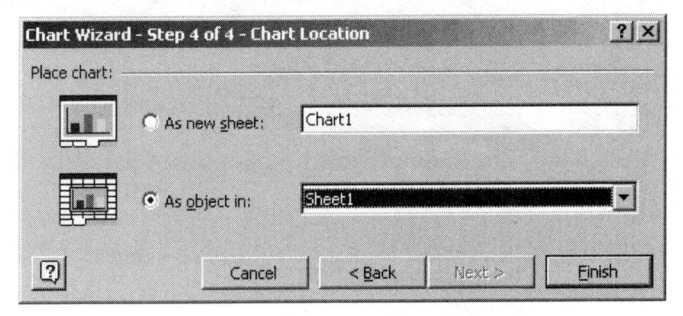

Figure C-5 The fourth Chart Wizard dialog box.

Customizing a Chart

To customize a chart, select the chart and then click the Chart Wizard toolbar button. Excel restarts the Chart Wizard, and you can step through the four dialog boxes (described earlier in the preceding paragraphs) to make your changes.

You can make changes not described in the earlier discussion of the Chart Wizard. For example, the Custom Types tab of the first Chart Wizard dialog box displays a variety of hybrid charts in which different data series use different data markers and also charts that use unusual color schemes (see Figure C-6). To use one of these custom chart types, select it from the list.

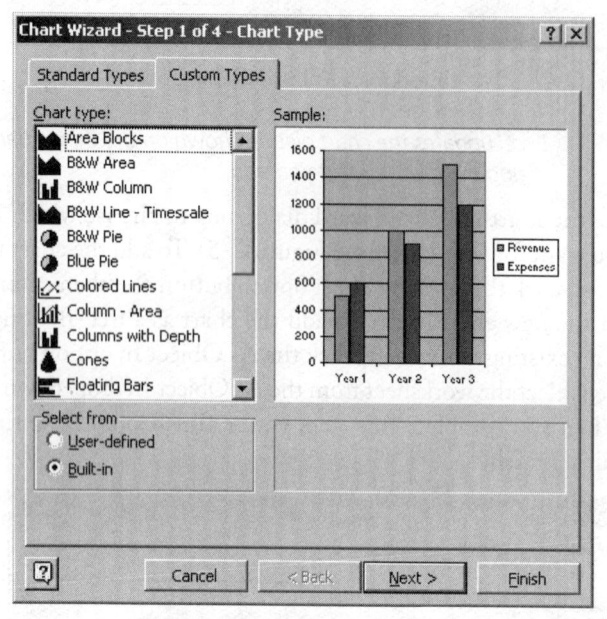

Figure C-6 The Custom Types tab of the first Chart Wizard dialog box.

NOTE *You can also change the chart type by clicking a chart and then choosing the Chart→Chart Type command.*

You can add to or change the data series plotted in a chart using the Series tab of the second Chart Wizard dialog box (see Figure C-7). To change a data series, click its name in the Series list box and then change the values in the Name and Values boxes. To add a data series to the chart, click Add, and then, after Excel adds the new series, use the Name and Values boxes to name the data series and identify the worksheet range holding the data series. To remove a data series, click the data series and then click Remove. The Series tab also provides a box you use to specify which worksheet range holds the data category names.

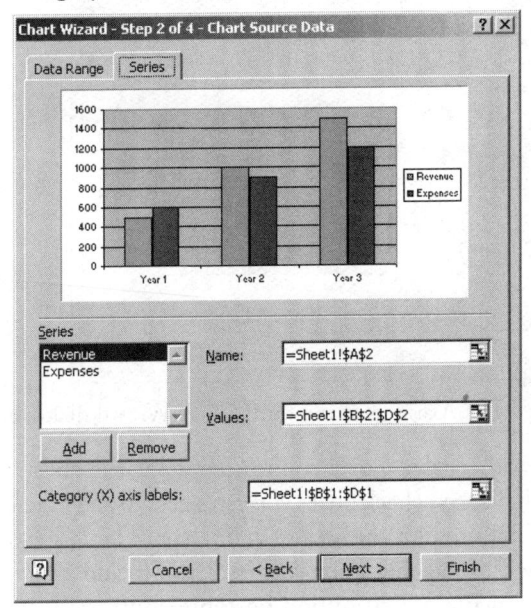

Figure C-7 The Series tab of the second Chart Wizard dialog box.

TIP   *If you click the worksheet button shown at the right end of the Name, Values, and Category (X) Axis Labels boxes, Excel minimizes the dialog box. You can then select the cell or worksheet range holding the name, to-be-plotted data, or data category names.*

NOTE *You can also change the chart type by clicking a chart and then choosing the Chart→Source Data command.*

You can use the third Chart Wizard dialog box, shown in Figure C-8, to change the text you've used to annotate the change, the appearance of the chart's axes, the gridlines used within the plot area, the location of a legend (and whether you even want one of these), whether data labels appear next to data markers, and whether a table of the plotted data also appears in the chart. For example, the Axes tab provides check boxes you can use to indicate whether you want a category and value axis and, for the category axis, what formatting you

Excel 2002 From A to Z

want. Rather than reading about what each of these options does, experiment with them yourself. If your experimentation still leaves you with questions, click the Question button in the dialog box's upper right corner and then click the option you have a question about.

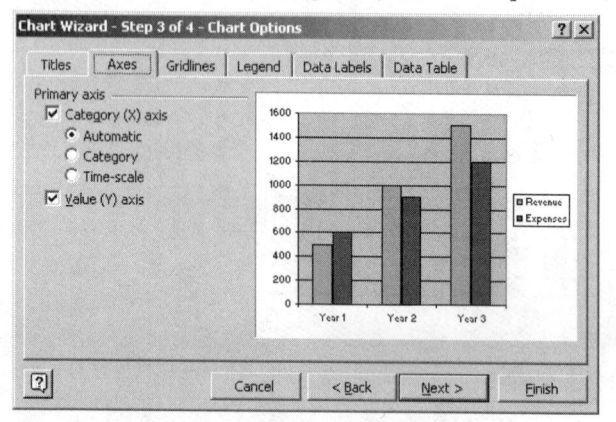

Figure C-8   The Axes tab of the third Chart Wizard dialog box.

Each of the other tabs allows you to customize the chart, too. The Gridlines tab displays check boxes you can select to add horizontal and vertical gridlines to plot the area of your chart. The Legend tab displays a Show Legend check box you can select to add a legend to the chart and then Placement option buttons—Bottom, Corner, Top, Right, or Left—which you can use to indicate where you want the legend placed. The Data Labels tab displays a set of option buttons you can use to indicate whether you want the actual data point values or equivalent percentages written next to their data markers. The Data Table tab provides check boxes that you can use to add a table and a legend of the data point values of the chart.

> NOTE   *You can also change the chart text, axes, gridlines, legend, data labels, or data table by clicking a chart and then choosing the Chart→Chart Options command.*

You can use the fourth Chart Wizard dialog box, to relocate a chart (see Figure C-9). To do this, simply select the other option button when you see this dialog box. For example, if the dialog box initially shows the As New Sheet option button selected, select the As Object In option button.

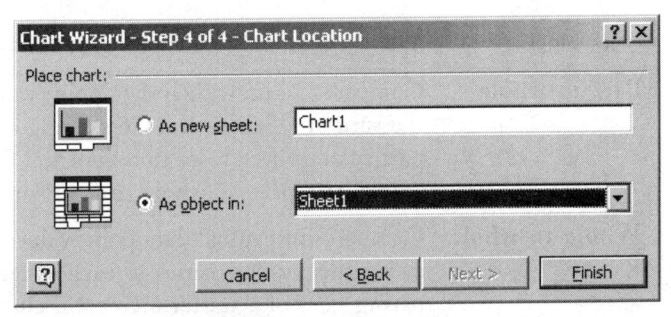

Figure C-9   The fourth Chart Wizard dialog box.

NOTE   *If you can't use the Chart Wizard or an equivalent command to change some element of a chart, you can right-click the part of the chart that you want to change and then choose the Format command from the shortcut menu.*

Resizing a Chart Object

You can resize any worksheet object, including a chart, by clicking the object and then dragging the square selection handles that appear on the sides and corners of the object.

Printing a Chart

To print the chart in the selected sheet, simply click the Print toolbar button or choose the File→Print command. To print a free-floating chart object, click it and then click the Print toolbar button or choose the File→Print command. You can also print the chart object by printing the worksheet over which it floats.

Choosing a Chart Type

Charts allow you to visually compare data in five basic ways, which means that your first step in determining the appropriate chart type is often simply to consider what data comparison you want to make. Suppose, for example, that you've collected detailed product sales revenue data for a golf equipment manufacturer. Using a chart, you might decide to look at this data in any of the ways summarized in the table that follows.

COMPARISON	DESCRIPTION
Part-to-whole	Compares an individual data point value to the sum of a data series. Comparing sales of a particular golf club set to total sales, for example, is a part-to-whole comparison.
Whole-to-whole	Compares individual data point values to each other or data series to each other. Comparing sales of a starter men's golf club set to a starter women's golf club set, for example, is a whole-to-whole comparison.
Time-series	Compares data point values from different time periods to show how values change over time. Showing monthly sales over the last year, for example, is a time-series comparison.
Correlation	Compares different data series to explore correlation between the data series. Comparing industry-wide sales to the average age of the population, for example, is a correlation comparison.
Geographic	Compares data values using a geographic map. Comparing sales by country, for example, is a geographic comparison.

Once you decide what data comparison you want to make, it's generally quite straightforward to identify the appropriate Excel chart types and sometimes even to identify appropriate chart sub-types.

- To make a part-to-whole comparison when working with just a single data series, you might choose a pie chart. (Pie charts plot only a single data series.) You might choose a doughnut chart or area chart if you're working with more than one data series.

- To make a whole-to-whole comparison, you might choose a chart that uses horizontal data markers, such as a bar chart or one of the cylinder, cone, or pyramid chart sub-types that uses a vertical data category axis and data markers. You might also choose a doughnut chart or radar chart.

- To make a time-series comparison, you would typically choose a chart that uses vertical data markers, such as a column chart, a line chart, or one of the cylinder, cone, or pyramid chart sub-types that uses a horizontal data category axis and data markers. You might also choose the stock chart if you're performing technical analysis of security prices. (Time-series charts typically use a horizontal data category axis because of the Western convention of using a horizontal axis to denote the passage of time.)
- To make a correlation comparison, you might choose the XY (scatter) chart if you're working with two data series or the bubble chart if you're working with three data series. You might also choose the surface chart if you want to explore trends in two dimensions.
- To make a geographic comparison, you would probably use the MapPoint program, which comes with Microsoft Office XP or, possibly, the surface chart.

Checking Spelling see Spelling

Clip Art

You can add simple drawings and images, called clip art, to your Excel workbooks. Microsoft Office supplies a rich set of clip art images through its clip art organizer. This organizer includes images that come with the Office suite of programs and images that you've collected in other ways, such as by downloading them from the Internet.

Listing Clip Art Images

To build a list of clip art images you want to use, follow these steps:

1. Choose the Insert→Picture→Clip Art command. Excel displays the Insert Clip Art task pane (see Figure C-10).

Figure C-10   The Insert Clip Art task pane.

2. Enter as much of the image's file name and extension as you know into the Search Text box. Use the ? wildcard in place of any characters you don't know and the * wildcard in place of any character sets you don't know.

3. Use the Search In box to specify where Excel should look for clip art.

4. Use the Results Should Be box to restrict the search to only specified types of clip art.

5. Click the Search button to begin the search. When Excel finishes, it displays a list of thumbnail images that match your search criteria.

Inserting a Clip Art Image

Once you build a list of the clip art images, click in the Excel workbook at the point where you want to insert the image and then click the image you want to insert (see Figure C-11).

Excel 2002 FROM A TO Z

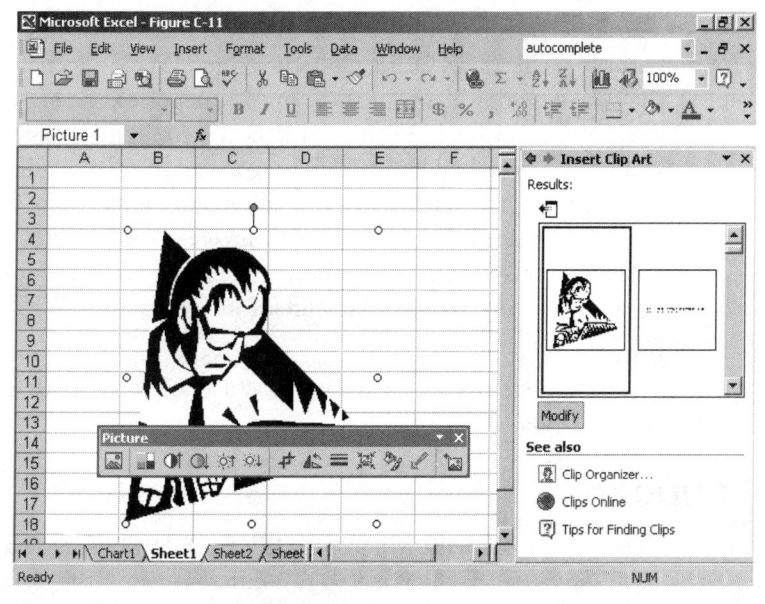

Figure C-11 An example of Excel clip art.

Using the Clip Organizer

The Clip Organizer works like an especially-tailored version of the My Computer window or Windows Explorer tool just for working with clip art (see Figure C-12).

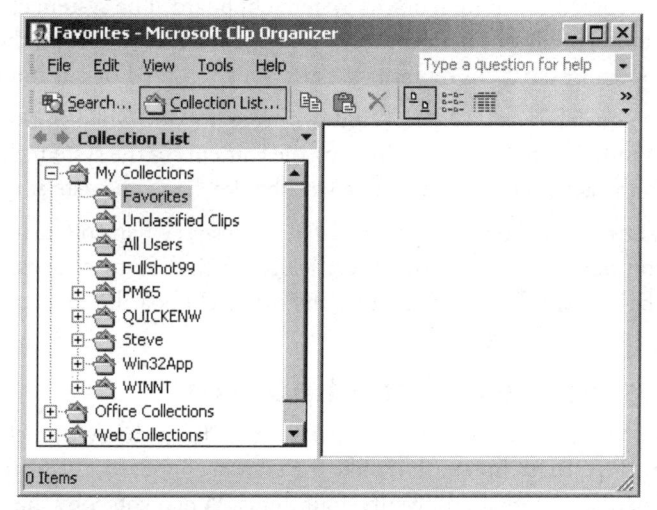

Figure C-12 The Clip Organizer window.

The Clip Organizer window organizes your images into three categories: My Collections, Office Collections, and Web Collections. To see the subcategories in any of these major categories, double-click the category folder icon. In Figure C-12, the My Collections folder is open and shows several additional subcategory folders. To see the images in a subcategory, double-click the subcategory folder icon. Clip Organizer displays a list of thumbnail images. You can right-click a thumbnail image to display a shortcut menu of commands useful for copying, moving and deleting clip art images.

NOTE   *The Clip Organizer toolbar provides many of the same toolbar buttons and tools as does the Windows Explorer or My Computer toolbar.*

Clipboard

When you work with Microsoft Office applications like Excel, the term *clipboard* actually refers to two different items: the system clipboard and the office clipboard. Both clipboards are temporary storage areas filled with items you cut and copy. However, the two clipboards work differently.

Using the System Clipboard

Whenever you copy or cut something in Windows, Windows stores the copied or cut item on the system clipboard. The system clipboard can store only one item at a time, so when you do copy or cut, the newly copied or cut item replaces the previously copied or cut item.

In non-Microsoft Office Windows programs and when working with Windows itself, you actually copy the contents of the system clipboard to the active window or active workbook when you paste some item.

The system clipboard gets erased in two ways: when you turn off your computer and when you specifically tell Office to clear the office clipboard. When Office clears the office clipboard, it also clears the system clipboard.

Using the Office Clipboard

In Microsoft Office, you can paste either from the system clipboard or the Office clipboard. Unlike the system clipboard, the Office clipboard can store up to twenty-four items. When you copy the twenty-fifth item, Office discards the first, or oldest, item.

To paste from the Office clipboard, first choose the Edit→Office Clipboard command so that the contents of the Office clipboard are listed in the task pane (see Figure C-13). Then, right-click the item and choose the Paste command from the shortcut menu.

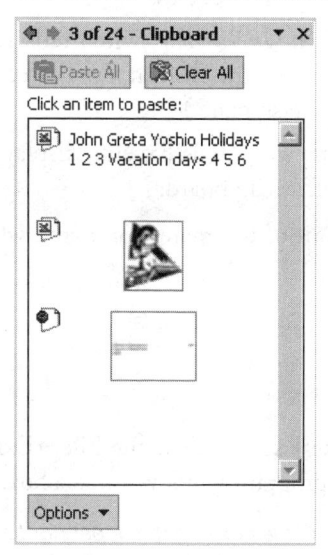

Figure C-13 The Clipboard task pane.

NOTE *To paste from the system clipboard, you choose the Edit→Paste command, click the Paste toolbar button, or use the Ctrl+V shortcut.*

The Office clipboard lets you copy items between Office documents and programs. For example, you can use the Office clipboard to copy an Excel chart to a Word document.

The Office clipboard gets erased when you close the last Office program. You can also erase the Office clipboard by clicking the Clear All button in the Clipboard task pane. (This also clears the system clipboard.) You can also erase individual items in the Office clipboard by right-clicking the item and choosing the Delete command.

Customizing the Office Clipboard

The Options button at the button of the Clipboard task pane displays a pop-up menu of four toggle switches you can use to control how the Office clipboard appears in the Excel program window:

- The *Show Office Clipboard Automatically* toggle switch tells Excel to display the Clipboard task pane when copying.
- The *Collect Without Showing Office Clipboard* switch tells Excel to collect copied items on the Office clipboard.
- The *Show Office Clipboard Icon On Taskbar* switch tells Excel to display an Office Clipboard icon on the Taskbar. (You can click this icon to display the Clipboard task pane.)
- The *Show Status Near Taskbar* switch tells Excel to display a message when copying to the Office clipboard.

Excel puts a check mark in front of the menu command when the switch is turned on.

SEE ALSO Copying Cell Contents, Copying Formulas

Closing Programs

To close, or exit, a program like Excel, choose the File→Exit command. Alternatively, click the program window's Close box.

NOTE *The program window's Close box is in the upper right corner of the program window and is marked with an "X."*

Closing Workbooks

To close a workbook, choose the File→Close command. Alternatively, click the workbook window's Close box.

NOTE *The document window's Close box is in the upper right corner of the program just beneath the program window's Close box. The program window's Close box is in the corner program window. Close boxes are marked with an "X."*

To close all the open workbooks, hold down the Shift key and choose the File→Close All command.

Coloring

You can add color or change the color of most parts of an Excel workbook.

Coloring Text

To color text, select the text. Then click the Font Color toolbar button's arrow to display a pop-up menu of colors. Click the color you want for the selected.

Alternatively, you can choose the Format→Cells command to display the Format Cells dialog box, click the Font tab and then use the Color list box to select a color (see Figure C-14).

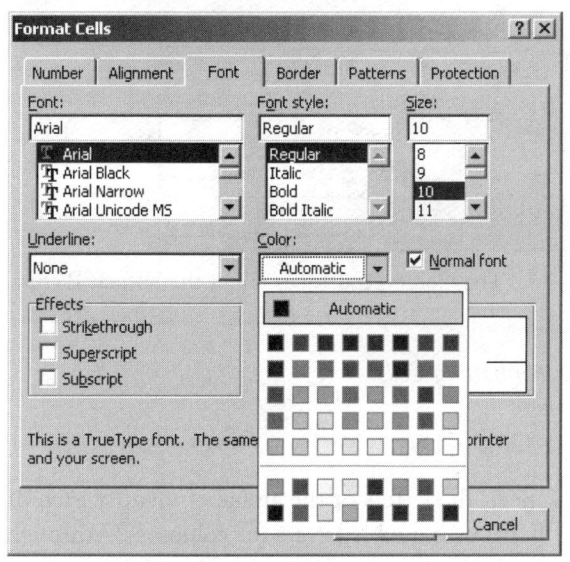

Figure C-14   The Format Cells dialog box.

Using a Fill Color for the Workbook Background

To fill the selected range with a color, click the Fill Color button on the Formatting toolbar. Then click the square that shows the color you want.

Coloring an Object

To color an object or some part of an object, right-click the object so that Excel displays the shortcuts menu. Choose the Format command so that Excel displays the Format dialog box. (The exact name of the command and dialog box will depend on the object you select.) Click the Colors And Lines tab and use the Fill Color and Line Color boxes to pick the color you want (see Figure C-15).

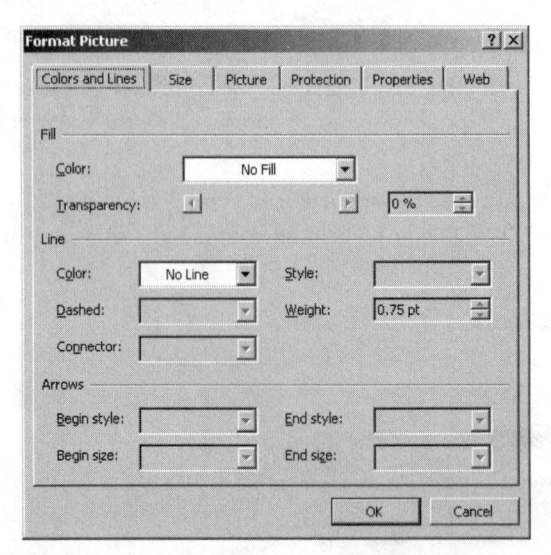

Figure C-15 The Colors And Lines tab of the Format Picture dialog box.

SEE ALSO *Formatting Cells*

Columns

In a worksheet, the letters of the alphabet identify each of the 256 columns. Excel uses double letters for columns 27 through 256.

To quickly increase the column width to accommodate all text in the column but include no extra white space, double-click the right border of that column heading.

To specify exact column width, select any cell in that column, choose the Format→Column→Width command. Enter the width in characters in the Column Width text box and click OK (see Figure C-16).

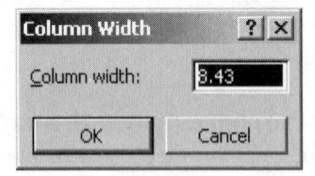

Figure C-16 The Column Width dialog box.

To hide a column, select any cell in the column and choose the Format→Column→ Hide command. To redisplay a hidden column, select a range that includes the columns to the left and right of the hidden column. Then choose the Format→Column →Unhide command.

Comments

To add a comment to the selected cell, choose the Insert→Comment command. When Excel opens a pop-up comment box, type your comment (see Figure C-17).

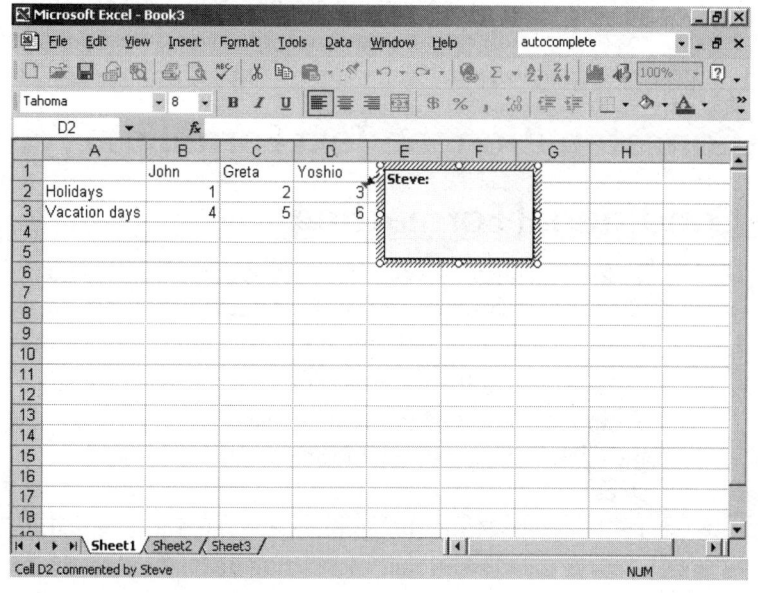

Figure C-17 A pop-up comment box.

To later view a comment, click the cell and choose the Insert→Edit Comment command. To delete a comment, click the cell and choose the Edit→Clear→Comment command.

Comparison Operators see Boolean Algebra

Computer Viruses

Excel workbooks can contain computer viruses because Excel workbooks can contain macros and Visual Basic programs. All someone has to do is write a mischievous or destructive macro or Visual Basic program and then have you open the workbook and run the program. For this reason, you'll want to be careful about opening strange workbook files. One way you can be careful is by disabling any macros or Visual Basic programs in strange workbooks you open. Excel, fortunately, will ask if you want to do this when you open a workbook.

Concatenation see Text Formulas

Conditional Formatting

To format only those cells that meet certain criteria, you can use Excel's Conditional Formatting feature. You might want to do this, for example, if you want to highlight cells in a budgeting worksheet that contain values larger than 200.

To apply conditional formatting, select the range of cells you want to include in the conditional formatting filters, and then follow these steps:

1. Choose the FormatÞConditional Formatting command. Excel displays the Conditional Formatting dialog box (see Figure C-18).

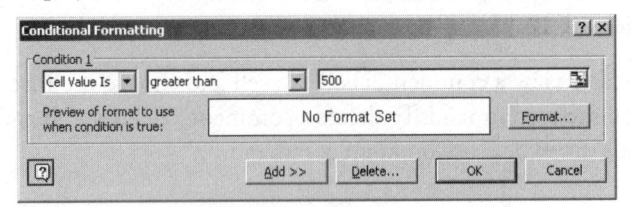

Figure C-18 The Conditional Formatting dialog box.

2. Enter the first criteria, using the drop-down list boxes and text boxes provided. For example, if you want Excel to display values greater than 500 in red italic boldface, indicate that you want to conditionally format cells with values greater than 500.

Excel 2002 FROM A TO Z   **C**

3. Click Format to describe how you want Excel to format the cells with contents that fit your criteria. When you do this, Excel displays a variant of the Format Cells dialog box (see Figure C-19). Use it specify the font, font size, font effects, and font color you want to use for cells that contain labels or values meeting your conditions. Click OK to close the Format Cells dialog box and return to the Conditional Formatting dialog box.

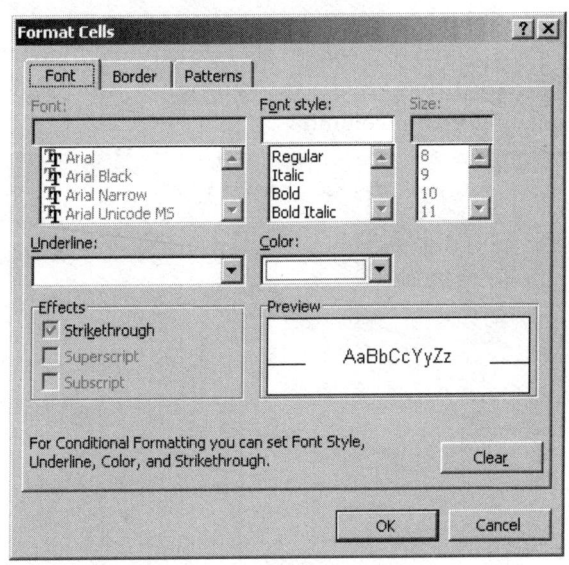

Figure C-19   The Format Cells dialog box.

4. Click Add, and Excel adds the conditional formatting rule. If you want to specify multiple criteria, repeat steps 1 and 2 for the other criteria.

5. Click OK, and Excel applies the conditional formatting.

SEE ALSO *Formatting Cells*

Control Menu

In the upper left corner of program windows, including the Excel program window, is an icon you can click to display the Control menu. The Control menu, a relic of the version of Windows that Microsoft sold a decade ago, supplies commands for moving, sizing and closing the program window.

33

Copying Cell Contents

You can copy the contents of cells and ranges and then paste them into other locations. This means you don't have to repeatedly type a label, value, or formula. You can type the entry just once and then copy or move it.

Suppose, for example, that the numbers shown in column C of a budgeting worksheet represent the budgeted expenses for January and that the same figures are projected for February and March (see Figure C-20). Rather than reenter the same values, you could copy the values already stored in column C.

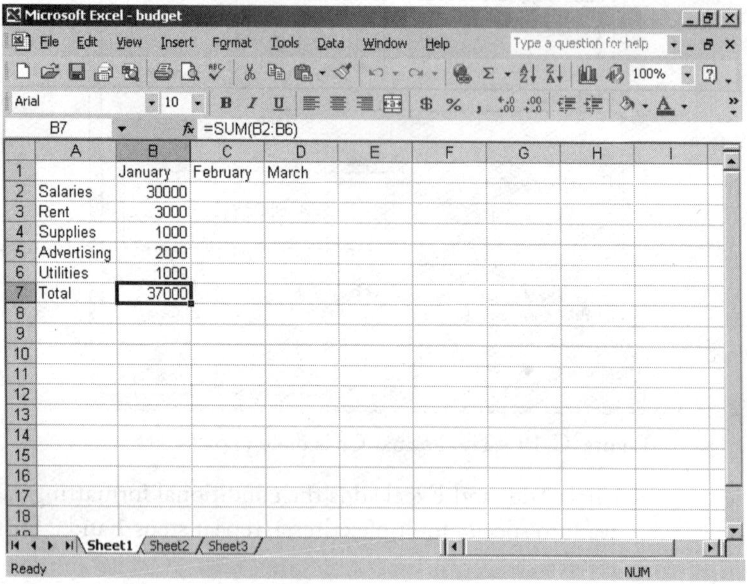

Figure C-20   The simple budgeting worksheet.

To copy the labels and values for such an operation, follow these steps:

1. Select the cell or range to be copied. The easiest method for selecting a specific cell or range is by clicking or clicking and dragging the mouse.
2. Click the Copy toolbar button, or choose the Edit→Copy command.

Excel 2002 From A to Z

3. Select the destination cell or the cell in the upper left corner of the destination range.

4. Click the Paste toolbar button, or choose the Edit→Paste command. Excel copies the worksheet range from the clipboard into the specified worksheet range (see Figure C-21).

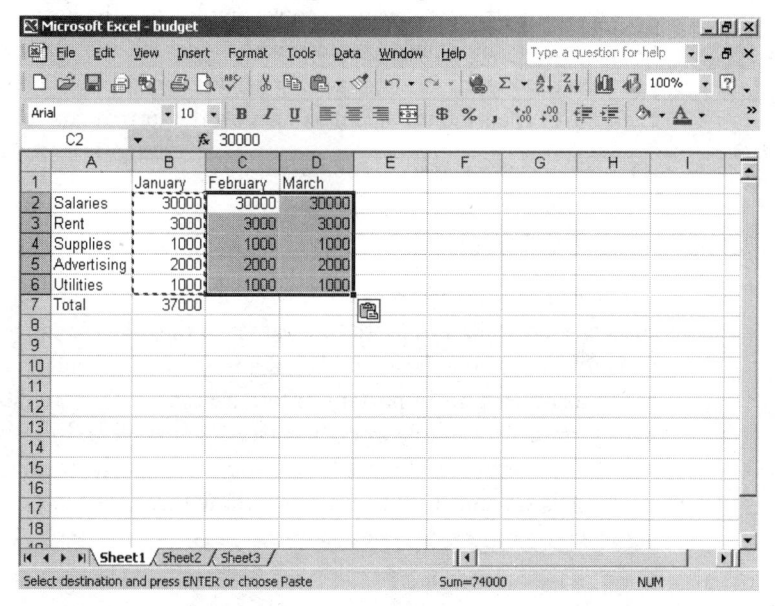

Figure C-21 A worksheet with the contents of B2:B6 pasted into the range C2:D6.

NOTE   *If you paste a copy of a single cell into a multiple-cell range, the contents of the cell are duplicated in each cell in the destination range.*

TIP   *You can also copy a cell or range with the mouse. Just select the cell or range, hold down the Ctrl key, point to the black border around the cell or range so that the mouse pointer changes from a cross to an arrow, and then drag the cell or range to a new location.*

SEE ALSO *Coping Formulas*

Copying Formatting

You can copy formatting by selecting the text, clicking the Format Painter toolbar button, and then selecting the text you want to format.

To format several ranges with the Format Painter tool, select the range with the formatting you want to copy, double-click the Format Painter toolbar button, and then go through your workbook selecting each range you want to copy the formatting to. When you format the last text chunk, click the Format Painter again to turn off the format copying.

SEE ALSO *Copying Ranges, Formatting Cells*

Copying Formulas

When you copy labels and values, Excel duplicates the contents of the copied cell or cells and pastes the data into the selected range. When you copy a formula, however, Excel adjusts any cell references used in the formula. This important difference can be illustrated by copying a formula in a simple worksheet (see Figure C-22). In a worksheet like the one shown in Figure C-22, you can copy the formula in cell B7 to cells C7 and D7. To do this, follow these steps:

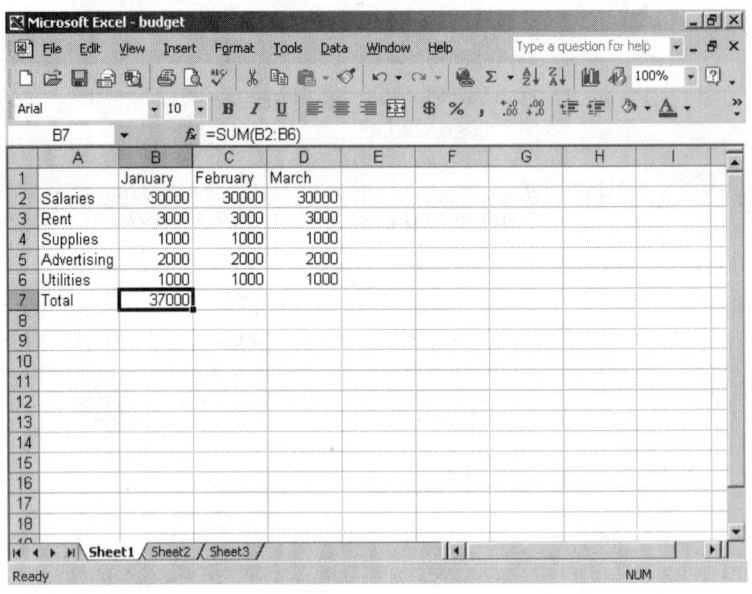

Figure C-22 A simple budgeting worksheet with a formula.

1. Select the cell or range with the formula(s) you want to copy. In the example worksheet shown in Figure C-22, you would select cell B7.
2. Click the Copy toolbar button. Excel moves a copy of the formula to the clipboard.
3. Select the destination range C7:D7.
4. Click the Paste toolbar button. Excel adjusts the formulas for the column in question and pastes the formula =SUM(C2:C6) into cell C7 and the formula =SUM(D2:D6) into cell D7 (see Figure C-23).

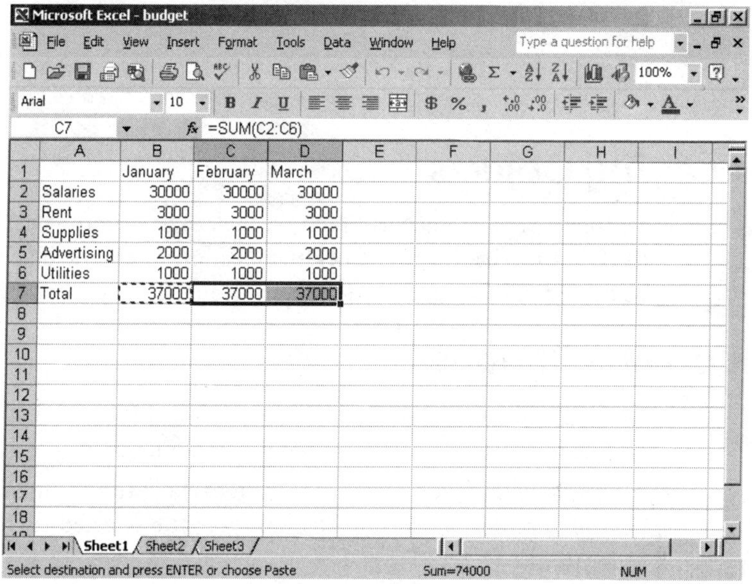

Figure C-23 The budgeting worksheet after copying the formula in cell B7 into cells C7 and D7.

The formula changes that Excel makes aren't a mistake. Excel assumes—unless you tell it otherwise—that the cell references in your formulas are *relative*. When Excel copies and pastes a formula with relative cell references, it adjusts them.

To prevent Excel from automatically adjusting the relative references of copied formulas, you can make them *absolute*. Simply place a dollar sign ($) in front of the part or parts you don't want Excel to adjust. For example, to tell Excel not to adjust the formula at all, place a dollar sign in front of both the column letter and row number like this, C2. To allow Excel to adjust row numbers but not column letters, put a dollar sign in front of the column letter but not the row number, like this: $C1. And to allow Excel to adjust column letters but not row numbers, put a dollar sign in front of the row number but not the column letter, like this: C$1.

TIP *If you press the F4 key while editing or writing a cell address, Excel toggles between relative, absolute and mixed cell references.*

Copying Objects

To copy an object, such as a picture, click the object to select it. Click the Copy toolbar button. Click the location where the object should be copied. Click the Paste toolbar button.

Copying Ranges

Excel provides several ways to copy worksheet ranges. To copy a range and its formatting, use any of the following methods:

- **Drag-and-drop.** Select text you want to copy with the mouse. Then, while holding down the Ctrl key, drag the selected text to a new location.
- **Edit→Copy and Edit→Paste commands.** Select the text, choose the Edit→Copy command, click the new location, and choose the Edit→Paste command.
- **Copy and Paste toolbar buttons.** Select the text, click the Copy button, click the new location, and choose the Paste toolbar button.
- **Office Clipboard task pane.** Select the text, click the Copy button or choose the Edit→Copy command, click new location, and click the item you want to copy in the Clipboard task pane. (If the Office Clipboard doesn't show, choose the Edit→Office Clipboard command.)

If you don't want to copy the formatting, choose the Edit→Paste Special command in place of the Paste toolbar button or the Edit→Paste command. When Excel displays the Paste Special dialog box, use the Paste buttons to specify what you want pasted (see Figure C-24).

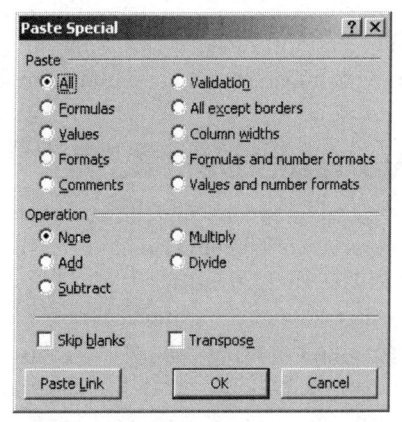

Figure C-24 The Paste Special dialog box.

SEE ALSO *Clipboard, Moving Text, Paste Special Dialog Box*

Currency Symbols see Formatting Cells

Cutting

You use the Cut toolbar button and the Edit→Cut command to move text, tables, and objects within and between workbooks.

SEE ALSO *Clipboard, Copying Cell Contents, Moving Cell Contents*

Database see Importing Databases, Lists

Data Categories see Charts

Data Markers see Charts

Data Points see Charts

Data Series see Charts

Data Tables

Excel lets you easily create simple data tables that show how changing a formula input affects the formula result. One-variable data tables let you experiment with how changing a single input variable can affect a formula's result or even several formulas' results. Two-variable data tables let you experiment with how changing two input variables can affect a single formula's result.

Creating One-Variable Data Tables

To set up a one-variable data table, you arrange the input values along either the left or top edge of a worksheet range and the formula or formulas you want to calculate along the other top or left edge (see Figure D-1). Along the other edge of the worksheet range, enter the formulas you want to test using the input values. In Figure D-1, for example, the worksheet shows two formulas for calculating the monthly mortgage payment.

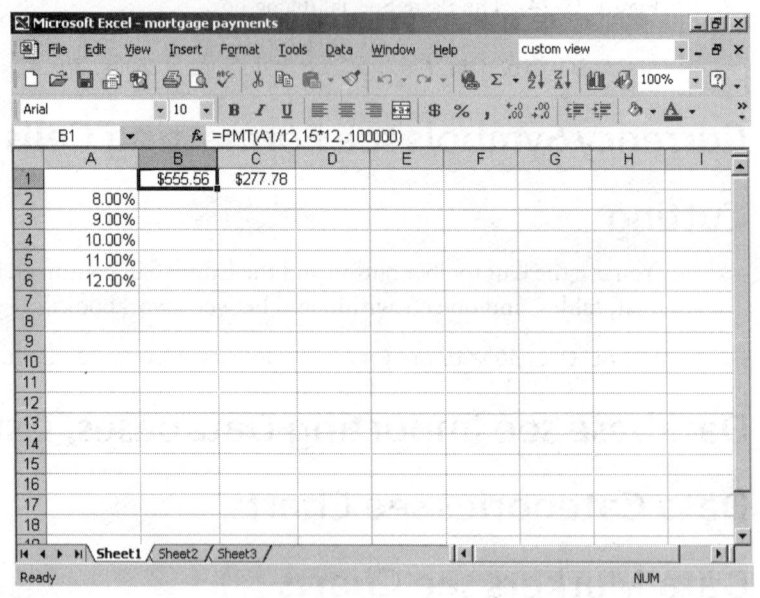

Figure D-1 An Excel worksheet range set up for creating a one-variable data table.

NOTE *The PMT function, which is used in the workbook shown in Figure D-1, uses the following syntax: PMT(rate,term,loan) in which* rate *is the periodic interest rate,* term *is the number of payments, and* loan *is the loan amount.*

Cell B1 holds the formula shown below to calculate the monthly payment on a 15-year, $100,000 mortgage:

=PMT(A1/12,15*12,-100000)

Cell C1 holds the formula shown below to calculate the monthly payment on a 30-year, $100,000 mortgage:

=PMT(A1/12,30*12,-100000)

The key point to note about both of these formulas—*this is the secret to using a one-variable data table*—is that they refer to the empty corner cell of the worksheet that holds the data table.

Once you've arranged the input values and the formulas, finish the data table by following these steps:

1. Select the worksheet range that includes the input values and the formulas.

2. Choose the Data→Table command. Excel displays the Table dialog box (see Figure D-2).

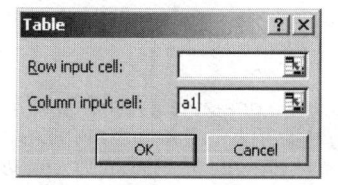

Figure D-2   The Table dialog box

3. Provide the input cell location. In the worksheet shown in Figure D-1, the two what-if formulas use cell A1 as the changing, interest-rate input value. So this is the input cell. Because Figure D-1 arranges the input values into a column, you enter this cell address in the Column Input Cell text box, as shown in Figure D-2.

4. Click OK. Excel fills the data table with formula results for each input value, (see Figure D-3). For example, Excel fills cell B2 by using the formula in cell B1 and the interest rate in cell A2 to calculate the monthly payment on a 15-year, $100,000 mortgage

when the annual interest rate is 8.00%. Excel fills cell C3 by using the formula in cell C1 and the interest rate in cell A3 to calculate the monthly payment on a 30-year, $100,000 mortgage when the annual interest rate is 9.00%.

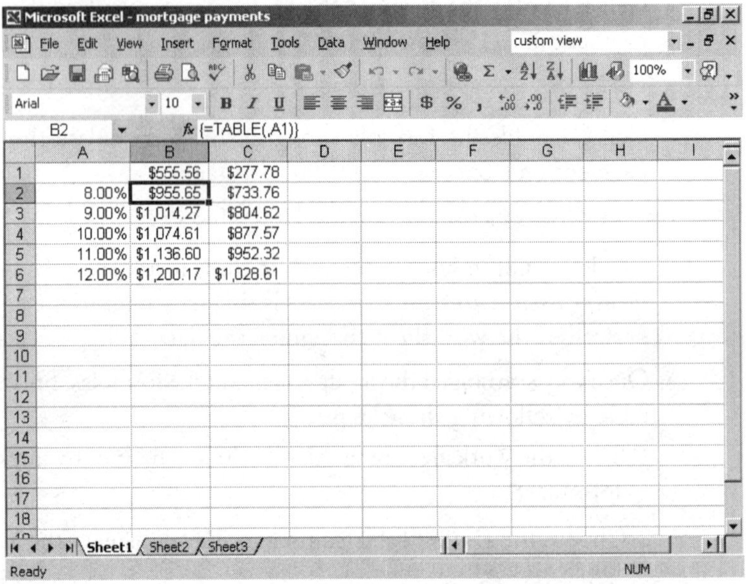

	A	B	C
1		$555.56	$277.78
2	8.00%	$955.65	$733.76
3	9.00%	$1,014.27	$804.62
4	10.00%	$1,074.61	$877.57
5	11.00%	$1,136.60	$952.32
6	12.00%	$1,200.17	$1,028.61

Cell B2 contains: {=TABLE(,A1)}

Figure D-3 The data table after calculating the what-if formula for each of the input values.

NOTE *Figures D-1 and D-3 show a one-variable data table that stores the input values along the left edge and the formulas along the top edge of the worksheet range. You can also store input values along the top edge and the formulas along the left edge. If you use this alternative organization, you enter the input cell address in the Table dialog box's Row Input Cell text box.*

After you set up the one-variable data table, you can continue your what-if analysis without having to use the Data→Table command. Simply change the input values. Excel updates the formula results for your changes.

Creating Two-Variable Data Tables

To set up a two-variable data table, you arrange the two sets of input values along the left and top edge of a worksheet range. You then place the what-if formula in the top-left corner cell of the worksheet range (see Figure D-4).

Excel 2002 FROM A TO Z

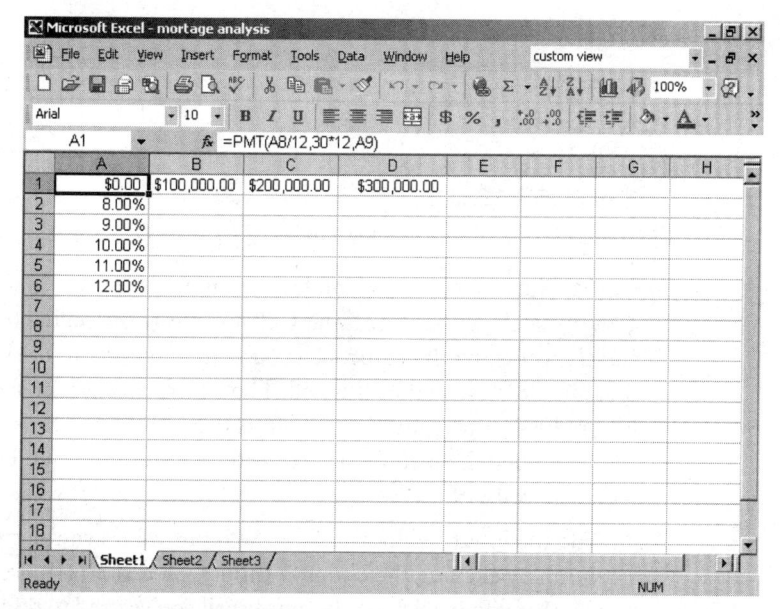

[Screenshot of Microsoft Excel - mortgage analysis worksheet. Cell A1 contains the formula =PMT(A8/12,30*12,A9) and displays $0.00. Row 1: A1=$0.00, B1=$100,000.00, C1=$200,000.00, D1=$300,000.00. Column A rows 2-6 contain: 8.00%, 9.00%, 10.00%, 11.00%, 12.00%.]

Figure D-4   An Excel worksheet range set up for creating a two-variable data table.

In Figure D-4, cell A1 holds the formula shown below to calculate the monthly payment on a 30-year mortgage:

`=PMT(A8/12,30*12,A9)`

NOTE   *The PMT function uses the syntax PMT(rate,term,loan) in which* rate *is the periodic interest rate,* term *is the number of payments, and* loan *is the loan amount.*

The key point to note about this formula—*and this is the secret to using a two-variable data table*—is that the formula refers to two empty cells below the worksheet range, A8 and A9, that will be used to store the what-if data.

Once you've arranged the input values and the formula, finish the data table by following these steps:

1. Select the worksheet range that includes the input values.

2. Choose the Data→Table command. Excel displays the Table dialog box (see Figure D-5).

43

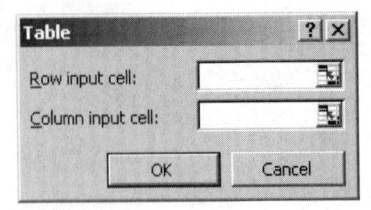

Figure D-5 The Table dialog box.

3. Provide the input cell location for the input values you've stored in a row by clicking the Row Input Cell text box (to select the text box) and then clicking the empty cell you've used to refer to the variable that should be stored in this cell. The simple worksheet shown in Figure D-4 stores mortgage amounts in a row, so you click the cell that the what-if formula uses to refer to the mortgage balance, which is cell A9.

4. Provide the input cell location for the input values you've stored in a column by clicking the Column Input Cell text box (to select the text box) and then clicking the empty cell you've used to refer to the variable that should be stored in this cell. The simple worksheet shown in Figure D-5 stores interest rates in a row, so you click the cell that the what-if formula uses to refer to the interest rates, which is cell A8.

5. Click OK. Excel fills the data table with formula results for each input value (see Figure D-6). For example, Excel fills cell B2 by using the formula in cell B1 and the interest rate in cell A2 to calculate the monthly payment on a $100,000 mortgage when the annual interest rate is 8.00%. Excel fills cell C3 by using the formula in cell C1 and the interest rate in cell A3 to calculate the monthly payment on a $200,000 mortgage when the annual interest rate is 9.00%. Excel fills cell D4 by using the formula in cell D1 and the interest rate in cell A4 to calculate the monthly payment on a $300,000 mortgage when the annual interest rate is 10.00%.

Excel 2002 FROM A TO Z   **D**

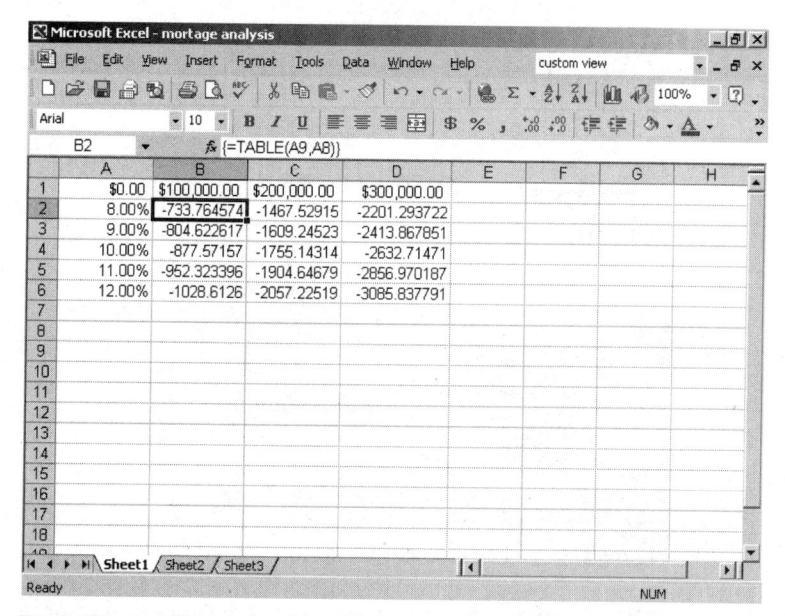

Figure D-6   The data table after you calculate the what-if formula for each of the input values.

As with a one-variable data table, you can continue your what-if analysis even after you've set up the two-variable data table—but without having to use the Data→Table command. Simply change the input values. Excel updates the formula results for your changes. In the worksheet shown in Figure D-6, for example, to see what loan payments would be using the same interest rates but with mortgage balances equal to $125,000, $150,000, and $175,000, simply enter these values in the worksheet range B1:D1.

Dates and Date Values

Excel uses date values to represent dates so you can easily perform date-based math. The value 1 represents January 1, 1900, the value 2 represents January 2, 1900, and so on.

To make date values easier to read, Excel supplies date formats, which you can see if you choose the Format→Cells command Click the Number tab, and select Date from the Category list box (see Figure D-7).

45

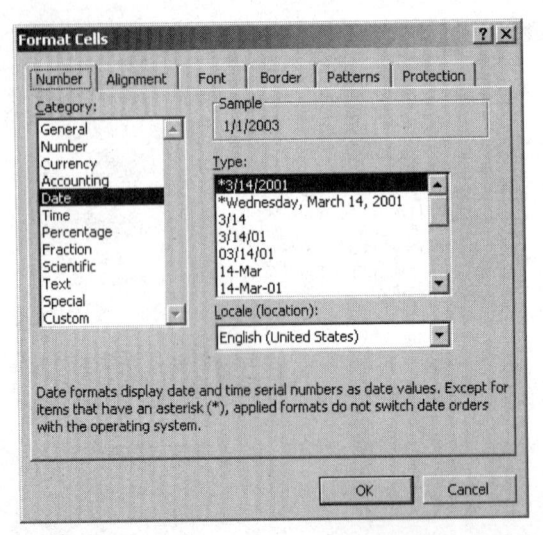

Figure D-7 The Number tab of the Format Cells dialog box.

> NOTE Excel uses decimal values for time values, so you can combine integer date values and decimal time values to create precise date and time values.

> NOTE Excel also assumes that anything you enter into a cell that looks like a date should be a date value.

SEE ALSO *Times and Time Values*

Decimal Values

To enter decimal values into worksheet cells, use the period as the decimal point.

SEE ALSO *Values*

Deleting Cells, Rows, Columns, and Worksheets

To delete a cell, range, row, or column, select the specific cell or range or any cell in the row or column you want to delete and choose the Edit→Delete command. Excel displays the Delete dialog box (see Figure D-8). Describe whether you want to shift the remaining cells up or to the left, or whether you want to delete the entire row or column, and click OK.

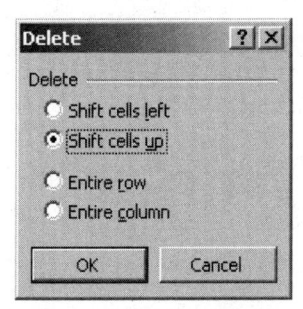

Figure D-8   The Delete dialog box.

Excel attempts to adjust the cell references and range definitions used in formulas for row and column deletions. For example, if a formula references column C and you delete column B so that column C becomes the new column B, Excel adjusts the formulas to reference column B. If you delete a cell referenced in a formula, however, Excel replaces the formula's reference with the error message #REF, indicating that the formula originally referenced a now-deleted cell.

SEE ALSO *Error Messages, Inserting Cells, Rows, Columns and Worksheets*

Delimited Text Files

Dependents see Formula Auditing

Detect and Repair

The Help→Detect And Repair command finds and fixes errors in the Office program files. To use this command, first find your Office or Excel installation CD. Then choose the command. Excel displays the Detect And Repair dialog box (see Figure D-9). Use the two check boxes on the Detect And Repair dialog box to specify whether you want your shortcuts to Office restored as part of the repair and whether you want your customized settings saved or want to revert to the default settings.

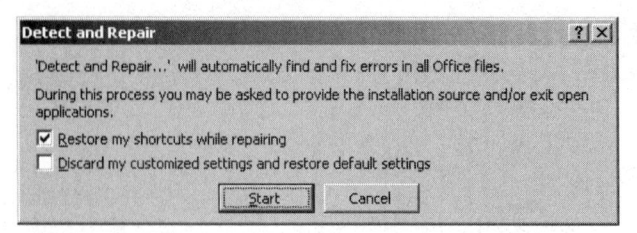

Figure D-9 The Detect and Repair dialog box.

Dictionary

Excel and other Office programs like Word use a dictionary, named CUSTOM.DIC, to check your spelling. You can add words to this dictionary by telling Excel when a word isn't misspelled but just unknown. To do this, you choose the Add command from the spelling shortcuts menu or click the Add To Dictionary button on the Spelling & Grammar dialog box. What happens in this case is that Excel inserts the word into the CUSTOM.DIC dictionary.

#DIV/0 see Error Messages

Document see Workbook

Drag-and-Drop

Drag-and-drop refers to copying or moving items with your mouse. For example, if you select a worksheet range, you can move the selection by dragging it to a new location. And if you select a worksheet range and hold down the Ctrl key, you can copy the selection by dragging it to a new location.

SEE ALSO *Copying Cell Contents, Moving Cell Contents*

Drawing

Excel includes a drawing tool which you can use to add lines, arrows, shapes and images to your workbooks. To begin drawing, display the Drawing toolbar by choosing the View→Toolbars→Drawing command (see Figure D-10).

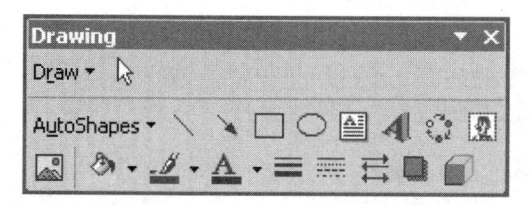

Figure D-10   The Drawing toolbar.

NOTE   *The Drawing toolbar can either be free-floating, as shown in Figure D-10, or it can be fixed. Typically, the Drawing toolbar is fixed and located along the bottom edge of the Excel program window.*

Drawing Lines, Arrows, Rectangles and Ovals

The Drawing toolbar includes buttons for drawing lines, arrows, rectangles (including squares) and ovals (including circles):

- To draw a line or arrow, click the Line or Arrow button. When Excel opens a drawing canvas, click at the point where your line or arrow should begin and drag the mouse to the point where the line or arrow should end.
- To draw a rectangle, click the Rectangle button. When Excel opens a drawing canvas, click at the point where the rectangle's top left corner should be and drag the mouse to the point where the rectangle's bottom right corner should be.
- To draw an oval, click the Oval button. When Excel opens a drawing canvas, click at the point where the oval's top left corner should be and drag the mouse to the point where the oval's bottom right corner should be.

TIP   *To make your rectangle a square or your oval a circle, hold down the Shift key as you drag the mouse.*

Drawing Text Boxes

A text box is a box into which you can enter text. To add a text box to your workbook or to a an existing workbook, click the Drawing toolbar's Text Box button, then click at the point where the text box's top left corner should be and drag the mouse to the point where the text box's bottom right corner should be. To make your text box square, hold down

D Excel 2002 From A to Z

the Shift key while you drag the mouse. After you draw your text box, type the text you want the box to hold (see Figure D-11).

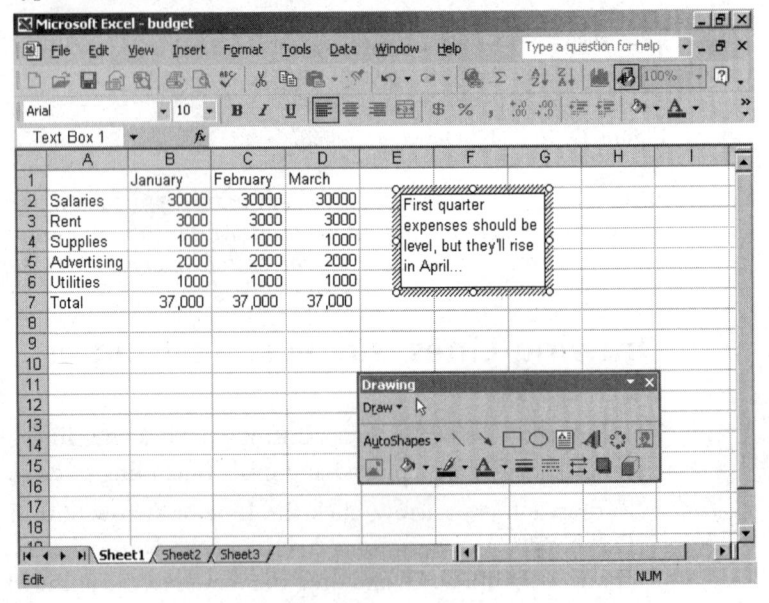

Figure D-11 A worksheet with a text box.

Drawing AutoShapes

The Drawing toolbar includes an AutoShapes tool which lets you draw dozens and dozens of common shapes such as hearts, stars, polygons, and flow chart symbols. To draw an autoshape, click the AutoShapes tool and then select one of the AutoShapes menu commands: Lines, Connectors (which are shapes that connect lines), Basic Shapes, Block Arrows, Stars And Banners, Callouts or More Shapes. When Excel displays a list of the autoshapes with the selected category, click the one you want to add and then drag the mouse to size and position the autoshape (see Figure D-12).

Excel 2002 From A to Z

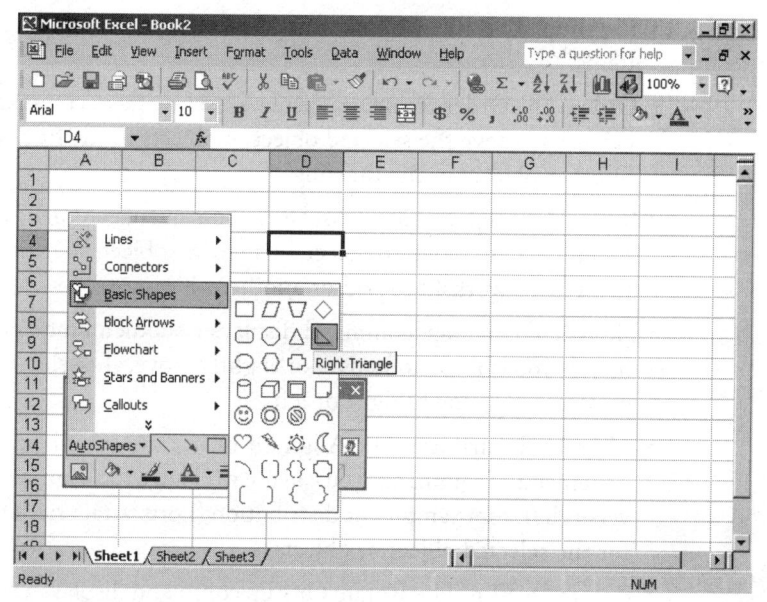

Figure D-12 A menu of autoshapes.

Selecting Objects

The Drawing toolbar's Select Objects button lets you select more than one drawing object. To select objects with the Drawing toolbar's Select Objects button, you have two selection methods available once you've clicked the Select Objects button:

- Hold down the Shift key and click the objects you want to select.
- Draw a rectangle that encompasses the shapes you want to select.

Working with the Draw Menu's Commands

The Draw menu, opened when you click the Draw button the Drawing toolbar, displays a dozen commands you can use if use the Drawing toolbar to create more complex drawings.

- **Group.** The Group command groups the selected objects so they can be moved, sized, and formatted as a group.
- **Ungroup.** The Ungroup command ungroups previously grouped items.

- **Regroup.** The Regroup command groups previously ungrouped items.
- **Order.** The Order command displays a submenu of commands you can use to move the selected object or objects to the front or back of other objects in the drawing.
- **Snap.** The Snap command displays a submenu of commands you use to tell Excel to move an object, or snap the object, so it aligns perfectly with worksheet grid or another object.
- **Nudge.** The Nudge command displays a submenu menu of commands you can use to nudge, or slightly move, the selected object or objects up, down, right or left.
- **Align Or Distribute.** The Align Or Distribute command displays a submenu of commands you can use to change the alignment (right versus left, for example) or distribution (horizontal versus vertical) for the selected object or objects.
- **Rotate Or Flip.** The Rotate Or Flip command displays a submenu of commands you can use to rotate an object and to horizontally or vertically flip an object.
- **Reroute Connectors.** The Reroute Connectors command lets you change where connectors connect.
- **Edit Points.** The Edit Points command lets you change the line used in a curve, a freeform shape or a scribble.
- **Change AutoShape.** The Change AutoShape command lets you change the autoshape of the selected autoshape object.
- **Set AutoShape Default.** The Set AutoShape Default command lets you pick the default autoshape used within each autoshape category.

Formatting Drawing Objects

You can usually change the appearance or format of a drawing object by right-clicking the object, choosing the Format AutoShape command from the shortcuts menu, and then using the dialog box that Excel displays to color the shape and its border, change the lines used to draw the shape, and add or remove patterns (see Figure D-13).

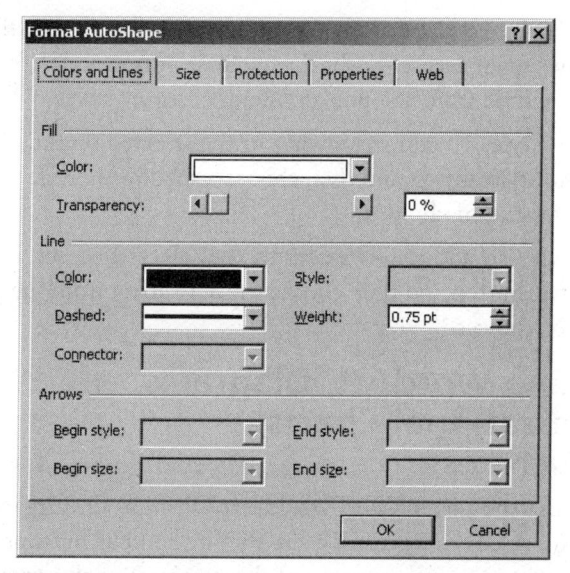

Figure D-13   The Colors And Lines tab of the Format AutoShape dialog box.

The Drawing toolbar also provides toolbar buttons for making common formatting changes to drawing objects:

- **Fill Color.**   To change the color of the selected item, click the Fill Color button's arrow and then choose the color you want from the pop-up menu of colors.

- **Line Color.**   To change the color of the selected line or arrow, click the Line Color button's arrow and choose the color from the pop-up menu of colors. Click the color you want for the line.

- **Font Color.**   To change the color of the selected text, click the Font Color button and then choose the color you want from the pop-up menu of colors.

- **Line Style.**   To change the weight of the selected line or arrow, click the Line Style button and then choose a line weight from the pop-up menu of line weights.

- **Dash Style.**   To change the selected solid line or arrow into a dashed line or arrow—or vice versus—click the Dash Style button and then choose a dashed line style from the pop-up menu of dashed line options.

- **Arrow Style.** To change the selected arrow's direction or the type of arrowhead it uses, click the Arrow Style button and then choose an arrow style from the pop-up menu of arrow styles.
- **Shadow Style.** To add shadowing to the selected object, click the Shadow Style button and then choose a shadowing style from the pop-up menu of choices.
- **3-D Style.** To add a 3-D effect to the selected object, click the 3-D Style button and then choose the 3-D effect from the pop-up menu of choices.

Inserting WordArt, Diagrams, Organizational Charts, and Pictures

You can use the Insert WordArt, Insert Diagram Or Organization Chart, Insert Clip Art, and Insert Picture toolbar buttons to add WordArt, diagrams, organizational charts, pieces of clip art and pictures to your drawing. To add any of these items, click the appropriate button and then identify the item using the dialog boxes that Excel provides.

SEE ALSO *Clip Art Pictures, WordArt*

Editing Cell Contents

Excel cells work like the fields, or boxes, you see elsewhere in Windows. This means that it's easy to correct mistakes. Before setting a label or value in a cell, for example, you can use the Backspace key to erase characters to the left of the insertion point (the cursor) and then retype the correct data. You can also reposition the insertion point in the formula bar with the arrow keys and erase characters to the right with the Delete key. If you don't want to enter the data shown on the formula bar in the active cell, click the Cancel button or press the Esc key.

If you make a mistake but don't realize it until you set the label or value in the cell, move the cell selector to the cell with the erroneous content. To replace the cell's contents entirely, enter a new label or value. To edit the cell's contents, either click the formula bar or double-click the cell. Edit the cell contents shown in the formula bar or in the editable text box. When the formula bar or editable text box over the cell shows the correct label or value, set it in the active cell by moving the cell selector to another cell, pressing the Enter key, or clicking the Enter button in the formula bar.

SEE ALSO *Deleting Cells, Rows, Columns, and Worksheets, Formula Bar*

E-Mail

You can e-mail the open Excel workbook by choosing the File→Send To→Mail Recipient (As Attachment) command. Excel opens your default e-mail client (this may be Microsoft Outlook or Microsoft Outlook Express), creates a new blank message and attaches the Excel workbook to the message. All you need to do is address the e-mail message, provide a subject and some message text, and click Send.

> TIP *You can also e-mail Excel workbooks starting from within your e-mail client. When you do this, you e-mail them in the same way as you e-mail any file—typically by clicking the Attachment button and then using a dialog box to find and identify the to-be-attached file.*

Embedding Objects

To embed an object, such as a picture or some item created by another program, choose the Insert→Object command so that Excel displays the Object dialog box.

Creating New Objects

To create a new object, click the Create New tab and then select the type of object you want to create from the Object Type list box (see Figure E-1). When you click OK, Windows opens the program that creates the selected object type so you can create the object. When you exit the creating program, Windows returns you to Excel and places the new object in your workbook.

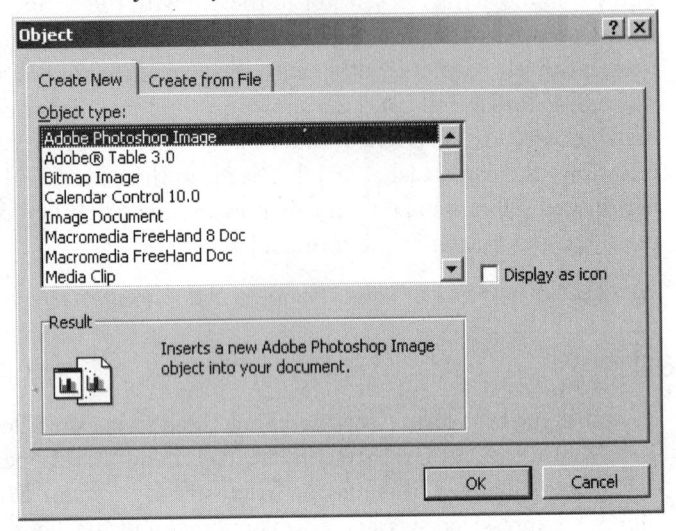

Figure E-1   The Create New tab of the Object dialog box.

Creating Objects from Files

To create an object by using an existing file, click the Create From File tab (see Figure E-2). Then enter the complete pathname for the file into the File Name box. If you don't know the complete pathname, click the Browse button to display the Browse window, which you can use to navigate through your computer's and network's folders and locate the file.

Excel 2002 From A to Z   E

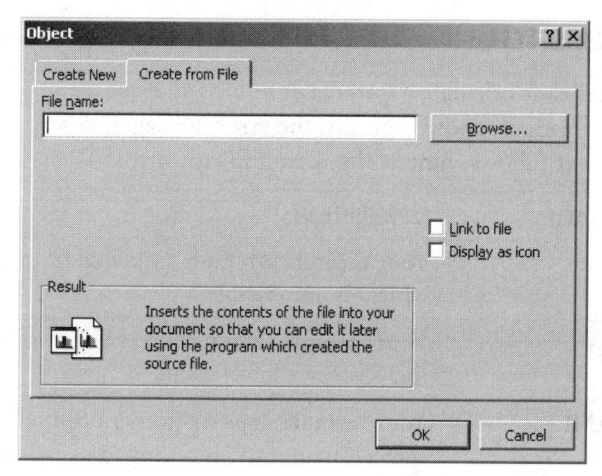

Figure E-2   The Create From File tab of the Object dialog box.

NOTE   *The Create From File tab includes two checkboxes you can use to further control how an embedded object works. Check the Link To File box to link the embedded object to the file that provides the object. (When you link, Excel alerts you to changes to the file and asks if the object should be updated.) Check the Display As Icon box to display an icon rather than a picture of the embedded object in the workbook.*

SEE ALSO   Pathname

Erasing Cell Contents

You can erase the contents and of the selected cell or a range by pressing the Delete key.

You can erase cell contents, formatting and cell comments by choosing the Edit→Clear command and the specifying what you want to erase. Choose one of the four commands from the submenu, as shown in following table:

COMMAND	DESCRIPTION
All	Erases all contents and formatting
Formats	Erases formatting but leaves contents.
Contents	Erases the contents but leaves the formatting.
Comments	Erases any comments inserted using the Insert menu's Comment command.

E

Excel 2002 From A to Z

Error Messages

If Excel can't calculate a formula, it returns an error message in place of the formula result. Typically, the error messages, described in the table that follows, hint at the reason for the error:

MESSAGE	DESCRIPTION
#DIV/0	Your formula attempts to divide by zero, which is impossible.
#N/A	Your formula references a cell that returns the "Not available" value.
#NAME?	Your formula appears to use a cell name but the cell name isn't recognized or is misspelled.
#NULL	Your formula attempts to provide value that doesn't exist.
#NUM!	Your formula attempts an impossible operation such as calculating the square root of a negative value.
#REF!	Your formula references a range that doesn't or no longer exists.
#VALUE!	Your formula tries to use text in a mathematical operation.

SEE ALSO *Formulas, Naming Cells and Ranges*

Exiting Excel

To exit Excel, choose the File→Exit command or click the Excel program window's Close box.

SEE ALSO *Closing Workbooks, Closing Programs*

Exporting

You can export text, worksheet ranges, and objects from Excel so they can be used in other programs and other workbooks. Probably the easiest way to export the selected text, a worksheet range, or an object is to choose Edit→Copy to copy the selection to the clipboard, open the new workbook or program into which you want to export the selection, and then choose the Edit→Paste command.

You can export an entire workbook by saving the file in a format that can be imported by the program to which you want to move the workbook. To do this, choose the File→Save As command. Save the workbook in the usual way—except use the Save As Type list box to choose a file format the importing program will recognize.

SEE ALSO *Clipboard, Copying Cell Contents, Lotus 1-2-3, Workbooks*

F4 Key see Copying Formulas

File Extensions

Windows appends a three-character file extension to your file name to identify the type of file. Excel workbooks, for example, use the file extension XLS. Typically, you don't enter the file extension for a workbook. Excel adds this automatically, based on the type of file you're creating or saving. Sometimes you can specify the file extension with the file name—and when you can your file extension determines the type of file Excel creates.

SEE ALSO *File names, Pathnames*

File Format

Different programs use different formats, or structures, for their files. The workbooks you create in Excel, for example, use a different format than the documents you create in Word (the word-processing program that comes with Microsoft Office).

By default, Excel 2002 and the two previous versions, Excel 2000 and Excel 97, use the same workbook format, but other spreadsheet programs and earlier versions of Excel use other formats.

You can choose which format Excel should use for a workbook when you save the workbook file. To do so, select the file format from the Save As Type list box, which appears on the Save dialog box.

SEE ALSO *Exporting, Workbooks*

File Names

You name your workbook by giving a file name using the Save or Save As dialog box and entering a name into the File Name box.

Your workbook name can be any valid file name, which means your file name can be up to 215 characters including spaces. All letters and numbers can used in file names. Some symbols can, but not the symbols that follow:

\ / : * ? " < > |

SEE ALSO *Workbooks*

File Properties

Excel and other Office programs collect information about the documents you create. You can view this information by choosing the File→Properties command. Excel displays the workbook properties dialog box (see Figure F-1). The workbook properties dialog box provides five tabs of information:

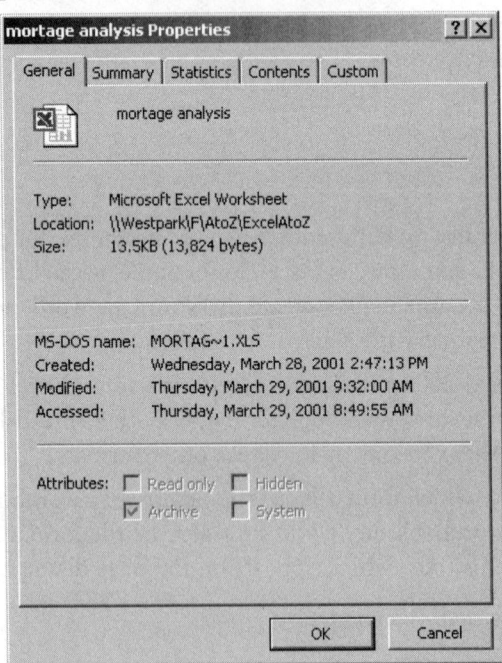

Figure F-1   The General tab of the workbook properties dialog box.

Excel 2002 From A to Z   F

- The General tab displays workbook name, location, size, and file attributes information.
- The Summary tab provides information and spaces to collect and store information about the workbook title, subject, author, and so forth.
- The Statistics tab reports when the workbook was last modified, opened, printed, and so on.
- The Contents tab lists the sheets in the workbook.
- The Custom tab lets you collect and store other pieces of workbook management information, such as when a workbook is complete, where it's been routed, and who the editor was.

Files see Workbooks
Fill Color see Coloring
Filling Cells

To continue a pattern you've begun, use the fill handle in the lower right corner of a cell or range. For example, if you begin the pattern 0, 5, 10 and want to continue it down a column, select the cells holding these values and click the little black square in the lower right corner of the range. The mouse pointer changes from a white outlined cross to a black cross. Now drag the mouse down the column as far as you want the pattern to go. This procedure also works for easily identifiable patterns of labels, such as months of the year and days of the week.

You can also copy a label, value or formula down, up, left or right in the selected rage using the Edit→Fill→Down, Edit→Fill→Up, Edit→Fill→Left, and Edit→Fill→Right commands.

If you choose the Edit→Fill→Series command, Excel displays the Series dialog box, which you can use to describe how Excel should fill the selected range (see Figure F-2). The Series dialog box lets you describe how Excel should create a series of values by, for example, adding 1 to the previous value or by multiplying the previous value by a percentage.

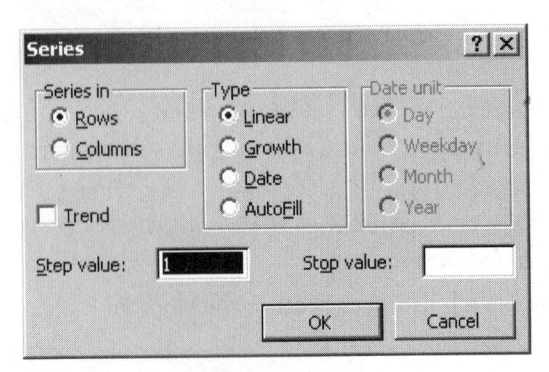

Figure F-2 The Series dialog box.

- Use the Series In buttons—Rows and Columns—to indicate whether the series should move across rows or down columns.
- Use the Step Value box to supply the value that gets added to the previous value or multiplied by the previous value to calculate the new value in the series.
- Use the Type buttons to indicate whether Excel calculates by new value by adding or multiplying or in some other way. Mark the Linear button to add the step value. Mark the Growth button to multiply the step value. Mark the Date button and then one of the Date Unit buttons if you want create a series of date values by adding the step value to a date value. Mark the AutoFill button to direct Excel to continue the series that you've already started in the selected range.
- Use the Stop Value box to specify at what value the series should end.

NOTE *If you check the Trend box and mark the Growth button, Excel doesn't use the step value to grow the series. Instead, it continues the growth rate shown in the first values of the selected range.*

SEE ALSO *Dates and Date Values*

Filtering Lists see Lists

Financial Functions see Functions

Finding Cells

To find cells or text within a workbook, choose the Edit→Find command. When Excel displays the Find And Replace dialog, enter the text you want to search for into the Find What box (see Figure F-3). Click the Find Next button to start Excel searching the workbook. If Excel finds the text, it selects the cell while leaving the File And Replace open. You can work in the workbook, including making changes in the selected cell. To continue searching, click the Find Next button again.

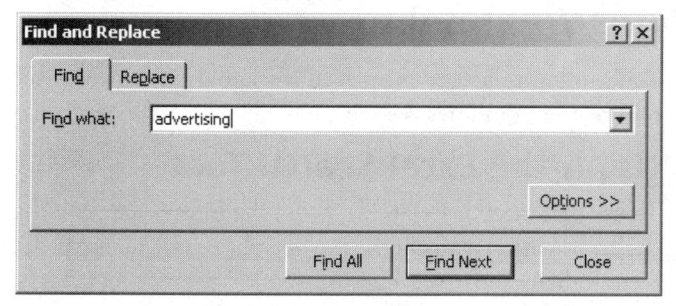

Figure F-3 The Find And Replace dialog box.

To search using more sophisticated search criteria, click the Options button. Excel displays an expanded version of the Find And Replace dialog box (see Figure F-4). Use its boxes to fine-tune your search criteria:

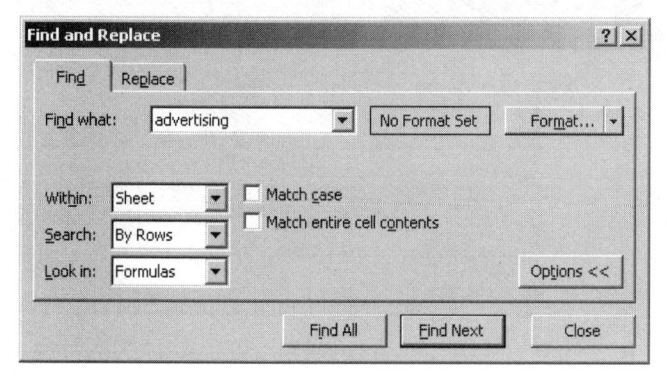

Figure F-4 The expanded Find And Replace dialog box.

- Use the Within box to indicate whether you want to search the active sheet or the workbook.

F   Excel 2002 From A to Z

- Use the Search list box to specify in which direction Excel should search.
- Use the Look In box to indicate whether you want Excel to search formulas, values or comments.
- Use the Match Case checkbox to indicate whether the case of your search text needs to exactly match the case of the workbook text.
- Use the Match Entire Cell Contents checkbox to indicate whether Excel should only find entire cell occurrences of the search text.

Finding Workbooks

You can locate lost or misplaced workbooks using the Excel Search tool or the Windows Search tool.

Using the Excel Search Tool

To use the Excel Search tool, choose the File→Open command, click the Tools button, and choose the Search command. Excel displays the Search dialog box (see Figure F-5).

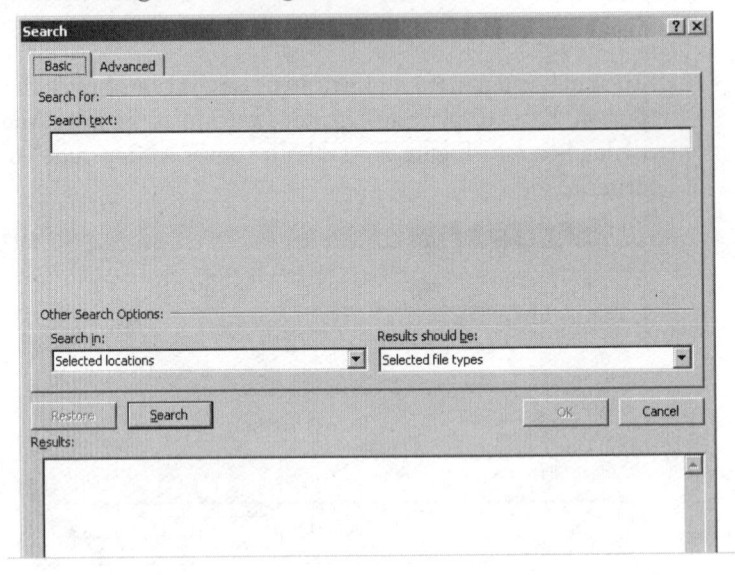

Figure F-5   The Basic tab of the Search dialog box.

If you know the file name, click the Basic tab and then follow these steps:

Excel 2002 From A to Z

1. Enter the file name into the Search For box. If you know a portion of the name, use that portion and the ? and * wildcards.

   TIP   *The ? character represents any single character (h?t finds any three letter filename that starts with an "h" and ends with a "t"). The * character represents any set of characters (June* finds any file name that starts with the word "June").*

2. Use the Search In box to specify on which drives Windows should look.
3. Use the Results Should Be list box to select which types of workbooks you're looking for.
4. Click the Search button. Windows begin searching for workbooks that match your search criteria. As Windows finds matching workbooks, it lists them.
5. To open a workbook in the Results list, double-click it.

If you don't know the file name but know something about the workbook's characteristics—such as what the workbook contains or who created the workbook—click the Advanced tab (see Figure F-6).

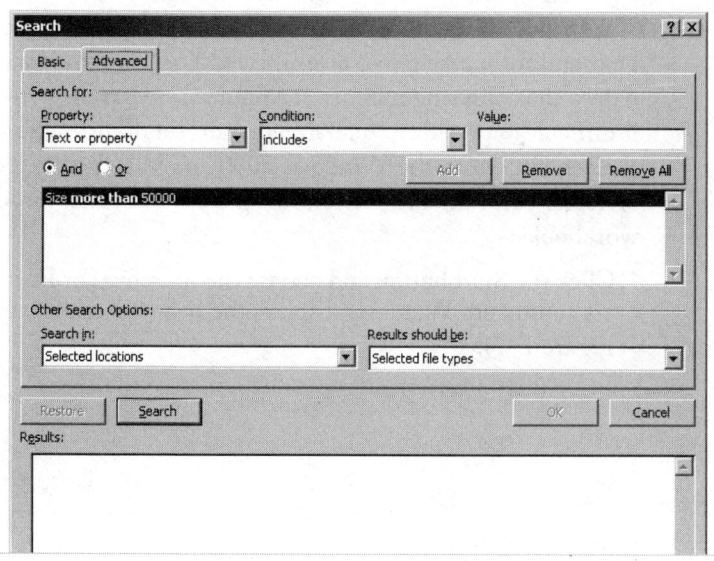

Figure F-6   The Advanced tab of the Search dialog box.

1. Use the Property list box, Condition list box, and Value list box to identify a file characteristic you can describe. For example, select Text

Or Property from the Property list if you know some the text contained in the workbook, and then select Includes from the Condition box and enter the search text into the Value box. As another example, select Size from the Property list box if you know something about the size of the workbook, then select one of the comparison operators (Equal To, Not Equal To, More Than, Less Than, At Least, At Most) from the Condition list box, and then enter the file size in bytes (not kilobytes) into the Value box.

2. Use the Search In box to specify on which drives Windows should look.

3. Use the Results Should Be list box to select which types of workbooks you're looking for.

4. Click the Search button. Windows begin searching for workbooks that match your search criteria. As Windows finds matching workbooks, it lists them.

5. To open a workbook in the Results list, double-click it.

Using the Windows Search Tool

The Windows operating system also provides a find file tool that can be useful for locating lost or misplaced Excel workbooks. Unfortunately, the confusing number of Windows operating systems makes it difficult to provide a "one-size-fits-all" set of instructions. Nevertheless, with both the Windows 2000 and Windows XP operating systems, you can take the following steps to search for and locate workbooks:

1. Click the Start button and choose the Search→For Files Or Folders command. Windows displays the Search Results window (see Figure F-7).

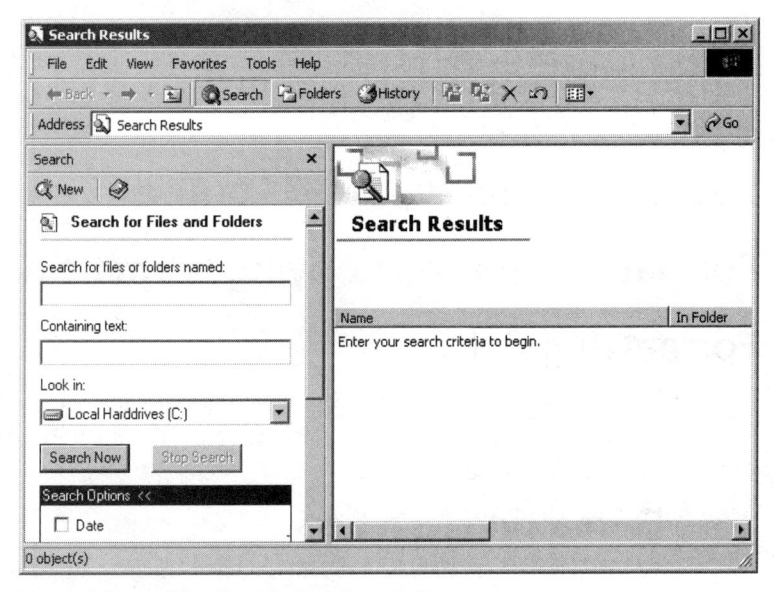

Figure F-7   The Search Results window.

2. If you know the filename, enter it into the Search For Files Or Folders Named box. If you know a portion of the name, use that portion and the ? and * wildcards.

3. To find files that use a word, phrase, or string of text, enter that word, phrase, or text string into the Containing Text box.

4. Use the Look In list box to specify on which drives Windows should look.

5. Optionally, use the Date, Type, Size and Advanced Options boxes to further refine the search. If you check one of these boxes, Windows displays other boxes and buttons you'll use to describe the criteria in detail.

6. Click the Search Now button. Windows begin searching for workbooks that match your search criteria. As Windows finds matching workbooks, it lists them.

7. To open a workbook in the Search Results window, double-click it.

> TIP   You can do other work with your computer while the search goes on. And you'll probably want to do this. Complex searches, such as those that look inside workbooks for matching text, can take a long time.

Footers see Headers and Footers

Format Painter see Copying Formatting

Formatting Cells

You can change the formatting of worksheet cells using with the Formatting toolbar (discussed in its own entry) or the Format→Cells command, described here.

Formatting Numbers

To format values in the selected range, choose the Format→Cells command and click the Number tab (see Figure F-8). Select the type of numeric formatting you want from the Category list box. Then, use the other boxes, buttons and lists that Excel displays to choose and fine-tune a number format.

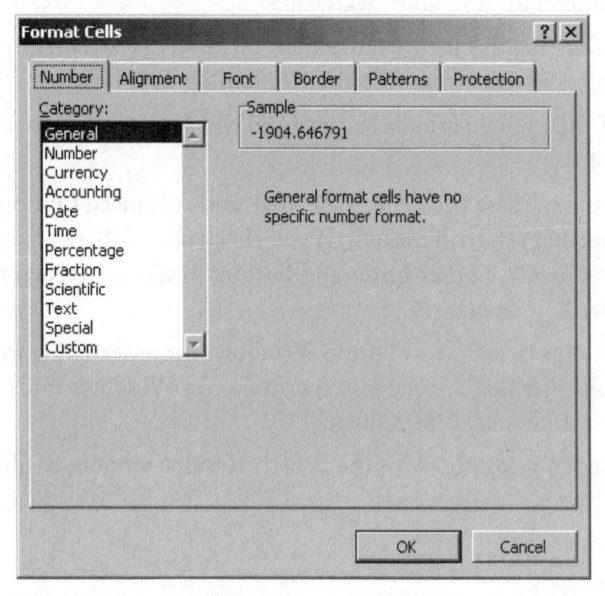

Figure F-8   The Number tab of the Format Cells dialog box.

NOTE Each category of number formatting has its own formatting options.

Adjusting Alignment

To adjust the way that labels and values are aligned in cells, choose the Format→Cells command and click the Alignment tab (see Figure F-9).

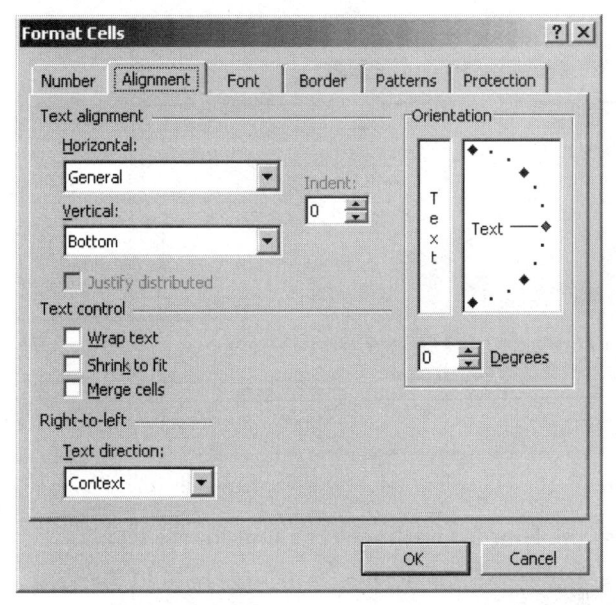

Figure F-9 The Alignment tab of the Format Cells dialog box.

- Use the Horizontal box to select how labels and values are horizontally positioned against the left and right edges of the cell. (The default General horizontal alignment tells Excel to left-justify text and right-justify values.)
- Use the Vertical box to select how labels and values are vertically positioned against the top and bottom edges of the cell.
- Use the Orientation boxes to change from the usual horizontal text orientation to a vertical orientation or something in-between.
- Use the Text Control checkboxes to wrap text to multiple lines, shrink the text, or combine selected cells.
- Use the Text Direction box to specify the reading order and alignment.

F   Excel 2002 From A to Z

Changing Fonts

To change the font, style, point size and font effects for the selected range, choose the Format→Cells command and click the Font tab (see Figure F-10).

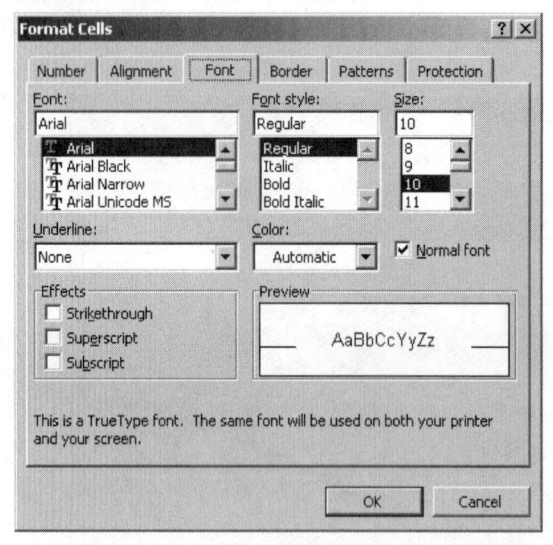

Figure F-10   The Font tab of the Format Cells dialog box.

- Use the Font list box to select a font for the text.
- Use the Font Style list box to italicize or bold the text.
- Use the Size list box to select a point size for the text.
- Use the Underline list box to add underlining.
- Use the Color box to select a color for the text.
- Use the Effects check boxes to add effects like superscripting and subscripting.

> TIP   *Remember that the Font tab's Preview area shows how your font specifications look.*

Adding Borders

To add a border to the selected range, choose the Format→Cells command and click the Border tab (see Figure F-11). You can use the Presets buttons to indicate you want borders around the outside border of the range or along interior rows of the range. Or, you can use the Border buttons to selectively add borders—including diagonal borders. The Line Style and Color boxes let you specify what the border lines should look like.

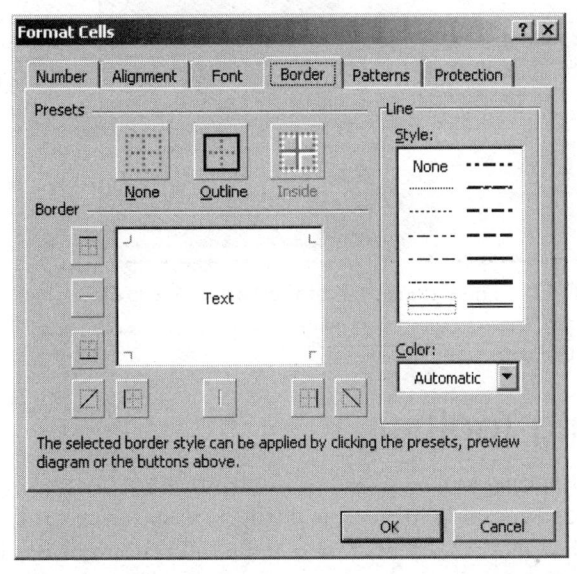

Figure F-11   The Border tab of the Format Cells dialog box.

Adding Shading and Patterns

To add shading or patterns to the selected range, choose the Format→Cells command and click the Patterns tab (see Figure F-12). Then click the color square that shows the shading color you want. Optionally, use the Pattern shading box to select a background pattern to go with the shading.

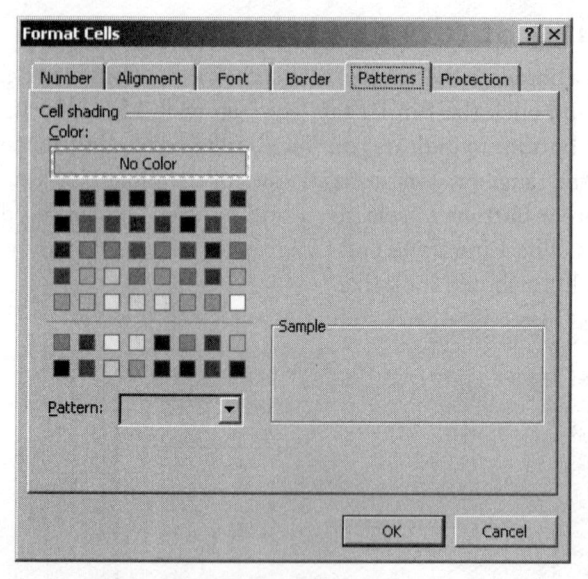

Figure F-12 The Patterns tab of the Format Cells dialog box.

SEE ALSO *Protection*

Formatting Toolbar

The Formatting toolbar provides buttons and boxes for making almost two-dozen common formatting changes, as shown in the list below. Note, though, that not all of these tools will appear on your Formatting toolbar. If you're using a personalized toolbar, only the formatting toolbar buttons that you most frequently use will appear. If you're working with the default Formatting toolbar, only the first seventeen tools listed will appear.

- The Font box lets you pick a font for the selected text.
- The Font Size box lets you a point size for in the selected range text.
- The Bold button adds and removes boldfacing to or from the selection.
- The Italic button italicizes and un-italicizes the selected text.
- The Underline button adds and removes underlining from the selected text.
- The Align Left button aligns the selected against the left page margin.
- The Center button horizontally centers the selected text on the page.

- The Align Right button aligns the selected text against the right page margin.
- The Merge And Center button combines the selected cells and then centers the text in the new merged cells.
- The Currency Style button applies the currency number format to the selection.
- The Percent Style button applies the percentage style number format (using two decimal places) to the selection.
- The Comma Style button applies the comma style number format to the selection.
- The Increase Decimal button increases the number of decimal places used to show values in the selection.
- The Decrease Decimal button decreases the number of decimal places used to show values in the selection.
- The Decrease Indent button un-indents the selected text.
- The Increase Indent button indents the selected text.
- The Border button adds a border to the selected line or paragraph. (If you click the Border button arrow, Excel displays a menu of border choices.)
- The Fill color button fills the selected range with a color.
- The Font Color button colors text in the selection.
- The AutoFormat button displays the AutoFormat dialog box so you can automatically format the selection.
- The Format Cells button displays the Format Cells dialog box so you can format the selection.
- The Increase Font Size button increases the size of the text in the selection to the next bigger size.
- The Decrease Font Size button decreases the size of the text in the selection to the next smaller size.
- The Left-to-Right button changes the text direction.

TIP   *To add a tool to the Formatting toolbar, click the down arrow at the right end of the toolbar. When Excel displays a list of the additional toolbar boxes and buttons you can add, click the tools you want.*

SEE ALSO *Personalized Menus and Toolbars*

Formula Auditing

The Tools→Formula Auditing command displays a submenu of commands that let you carefully check the way your formulas work:

- The Trace Precedents command shows which cells supply values to the selected cell's formula.
- The Trace Dependents command shows which cells use the selected cell's formula results.
- The Trace Errors command shows which cells supply the error-causing values to the selected cell's erroneous formula.
- The Remove All Arrows command removes the arrows that Excel draws to show precedents, dependents, and errors.
- The Evaluate Formula command displays the Evaluate Formula dialog box, which you can use to calculate parts of the formula and see intermediate calculation results.
- The Show Watch Window command displays the Watch Window which lets you build a list of cells whose formula results you want to monitor. (To add a cell's formula to the list, click the cell and then the Add Watch button.)
- The Formula Auditing Mode command is a toggle switch that turns on and off the auditing mode. In auditing mode, Excel displays formulas in cells not formula results. In addition, Excel draws colored borders around the active cell's precedent cells.
- The Show Formula Auditing Toolbar command opens a toolbar of commands for tracing precedents, dependents, and errors and for performing other similar audits.

SEE ALSO *Error Messages, Formulas*

Formulas Bar

The Formula bar shows the contents of the active cell (see Figure F-13). If the active cell contains a formula, for example, the formula bar shows the formula rather than the formula result.

To edit the cell contents shown in the formula bar, click the formula bar and make your changes.

Excel 2002 From A to Z   **F**

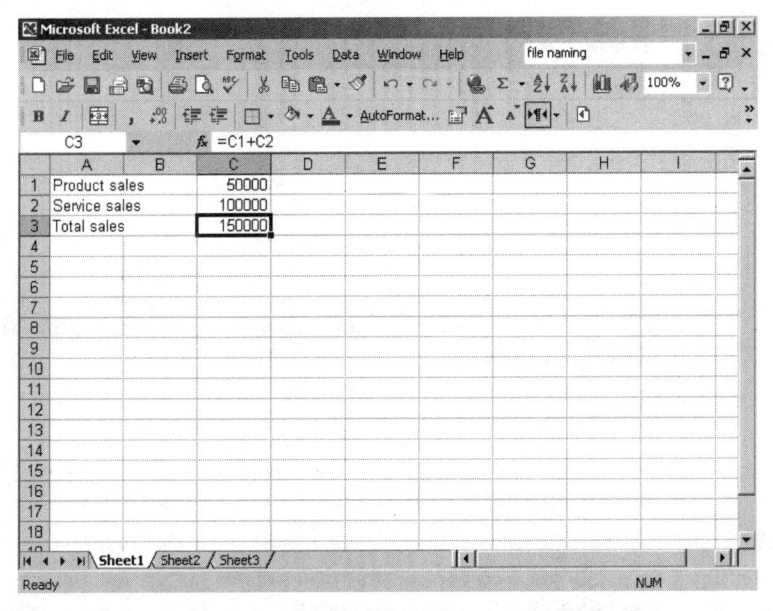

Figure F-13   The formula bar showing the contents of the active cell.

Formulas

Excel's power stems from its ability to perform calculations on the values you store in workbook cells using formulas you enter in other workbook cells.

Entering Formulas

You enter formulas into a cell in the same way you enter labels and values. With a formula, however, Excel displays not the formula, but its result. For example, if you enter a formula that says to add 4 and 2, Excel stores the formula in the cell, but displays the result, 6, in the worksheet.

Formulas must begin with the equal sign (=) or the plus symbol (+); that's how Excel distinguishes them from values and labels. You can construct formulas that subtract, multiply, divide, and exponentiate. The – symbol means subtraction, the * means multiplication, the / means division, and the ^ means an exponential operation. The table that follows shows the different mathematical operators and the results they return.

F Excel 2002 From A to Z

FORMULA ENTERED	RESULT DISPLAYED IN CELL
=4+2	6
=4-2	2
=4*2	8
=4/2	2
=4^2	16

To build more complicated formulas, you need to recognize the standard rules of operator precedence: Excel first performs exponential operations, then multiplication and division operations, and finally, addition and subtraction. For example, in the formula =1+2*3^4, Excel first raises 3 to the fourth power to get 81. It then multiplies this value by 2 to get 162. Finally, it adds 1 to this value to get 163.

To override rules of precedence, use parentheses, as shown in the table that follows. You can use multiple sets of parentheses in a formula if needed. Excel first performs the function in the innermost set of parentheses.

FORMULA ENTERED	RESULT DISPLAYED IN CELL
=1+2*3^4	163
=(1+2)*3^4	243
=((1+2)*3)^4	6561

Using Cell References

Excel allows you to use cell references in formulas. When a formula includes a cell reference, Excel uses the value that cell contains. For example, the formula =C1+C2 adds the values in cells C1 and C2.

To reference a cell on the same worksheet as the formula, you need to supply only the column-letter-and-row-number cell reference. To reference cell C1 on the same worksheet, for example, you enter *C1*.

You can also reference cells on other worksheets. To reference a cell on another worksheet in the same workbook, you need to precede the cell reference with the name of the worksheet and an exclamation point symbol. To reference cell C1 on the worksheet named Sheet2, for example, you enter *Sheet2!C1*.

You can reference cells in other workbooks, too. To do this most easily, open the other workbooks, begin building your formula as described earlier in this chapter, and then click the other workbook cell you want to reference at the point you want to include the reference. Excel then writes the full cell reference for you, which includes the workbook name. An external reference to cell C1 on the worksheet named Sheet2 in the workbook named Budget might be written as *[Budget.xls]Sheet2!C1*.

Formula Errors

When you build an illogical or unsolvable formula, Excel may display an error message in the cell rather than calculating the result. The error message, which begins with the # symbol, describes the error. Suppose, for example, that you enter the formula =1/0 in a cell. Because division by zero is an undefined mathematical operation, Excel can't solve the formula. To alert you to this, Excel displays the error message #DIV/0!.

Another common error is a circular reference. This occurs when two or more formulas indirectly depend on one another to achieve a result. For example, if the formula in cell A1 is =A2 and the formula in cell A2 is =A1+A3+A4, A1 depends on A2 and A2 depends on A1. Excel displays a warning and the Circular Reference toolbar when you create a circular reference. Excel identifies circular references by displaying the word *Circular* on the status bar and showing the address of the cell whose formula completed the "circle." It also draws arrows between the cells causing the circle.

To fix a formula error, move the cell selector to the cell holding the formula, click the formula bar, and edit the formula.

> **NOTE** *When a formula refers to a cell that contains an erroneous formula, both formulas return the error message. For example, if cell A1 attempts to divide by zero and cell A2 refers to cell A1, cell A2 returns the error message #DIV/0! as well.*

Natural Language Formulas

Excel lets you create natural language formulas in two ways.

One way is to name the cells you want to use in formulas. Do this and you can construct formulas that look like =Mortgage_Balance*Interest_Rate to calculate amounts such as interest charges. In this example, the cell holding the mortgage balance amount would be named Mortgage_Balance and the cell holding the interest rate would be named Interest_Rate.

Another way to create natural language formulas is to use labels in formulas. To use the label approach, first choose the Tools→Options command click the calculation tab, check the Accept Labels In Formulas box. Once you've done this, you can use column and row labels that clearly identify the cells in formulas (see Figure F-14).

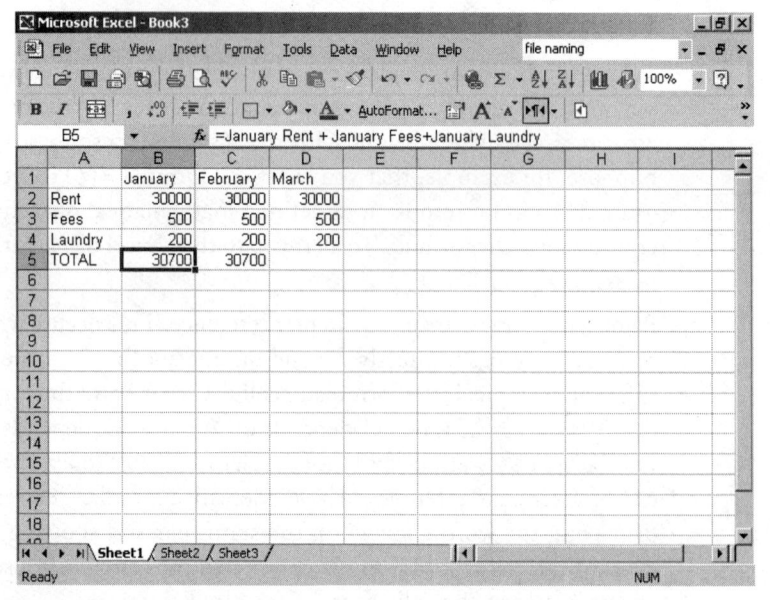

Figure F-14 A simple worksheet that uses label-based natural language formulas.

In the worksheet shown, for example, the formula in cell B5 that adds the contents of cells B2, B3, and B4 is:

=January Rent + January Fees + January Laundry

The formula in cell C5 that adds the February expense numbers is:

=SUM(February)

> SEE ALSO   Boolean Algebra, Error Messages, Formula Auditing, Functions, Naming Cells and Ranges

Fractions

Excel doesn't provide an easy way to display formulas as fractions. You can however enter fractions into cells and use fractions in formulas. To enter the fraction one-fourth into a cell, for example, type:

=1/4

To use the fraction 11/16ths in a formula, simply enclose the fraction in parenthesis:

=(11/16)*500

SEE ALSO *Formulas*

Freezing Window Panes see Window Panes

Full Size

Choose the View→Full Screen command to display an Excel program window that shows only your workbook and the menu bar but not the title bar, toolbars or status bar (see Figure F-15).

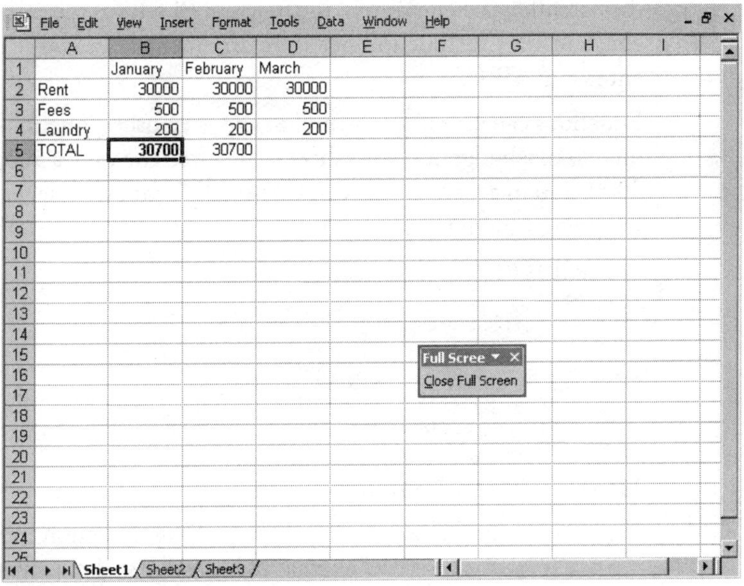

Figure F-15   The Full Screen view.

To return to the Normal view, click the Close Full Screen button, which appears when you're working in Full Screen view. Or choose the View→Normal command.

Functions

Excel provides more than three hundred pre-built financial, statistical, mathematical, trigonometric, and engineering formulas, called functions, that ease construction of complicated or lengthy formulas.

How Functions Work

Each function has a name that describes its operation. The function that adds values is named SUM, for example, and the function that calculates an arithmetic mean, or average, is named AVERAGE.

Most functions require arguments, or input values, which you enclose in parentheses. The ROUND function, for example, rounds a specific value to a specified number of decimal places. To round the value 5.75 to the nearest tenth, you could use the function shown below:

```
=ROUND(5.75,1)
```

Even if a function doesn't require arguments, you still need to include the parentheses. For example, the function PI returns the mathematical constant Pi. The function needs no arguments, but you still need to enter it as =PI().

Functions can use values, formulas, and even other functions as arguments. In a budgeting worksheet that stored the values 500, 50, 500, 2000, 250 in cells C1, C2, C3, C4, and C5, for example, each of the following functions returns the same result.

```
=SUM(C1:C5)

=SUM(C1,C2,C3,C4,C5)

=SUM(500,50,500,2000,250)

=SUM(SUM(C1),SUM(C2),SUM(C3),SUM(C4),SUM(C5))
```

Using Functions

To use a function in a formula, click the Paste Function toolbar button or choose the Insert→Function command. Excel displays the Insert Function dialog box (see Figure F-16). You can look for a function

Excel 2002 From A to Z

in two ways. You can type a description of what you want to calculate into the Search For Function box. Or you can select a category of functions from the Or Select A Category box. Excel then lists functions that calculate what you want or that fall into the selected category in the Select A Function box. Excel describes what the selected function does at the bottom of the Insert Function dialog box. When you have found the function you want to use, click OK.

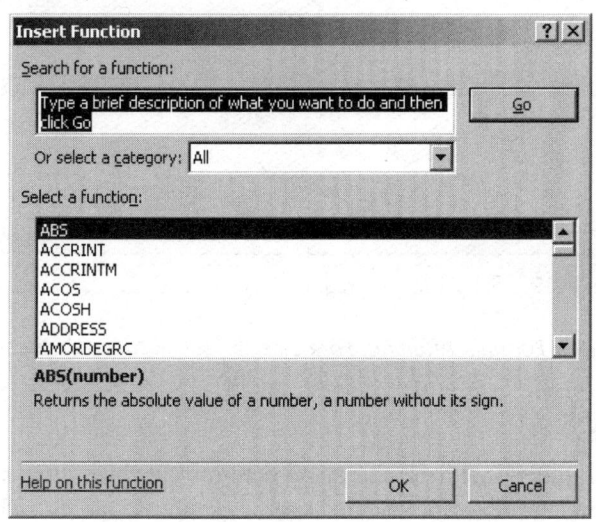

Figure F-16 The first Insert Function dialog box.

Excel displays the Function Arguments dialog box with text boxes you can use to identify or supply the arguments required for the function (see Figure F-17). If necessary, drag this dialog box to another portion of your screen to see the cells you want to include in the function. To enter cell data in an argument text box, click that box and then enter a value or select the cell or range of cells in your worksheet that goes in the box. Excel highlights the cell or cells you selected with a flashing box. To enter value or cell data in another argument text box, click that box and enter the value or select the cell or range in your worksheet that contains the data required for that box. Click OK when you're finished. Excel pastes the function in the cell.

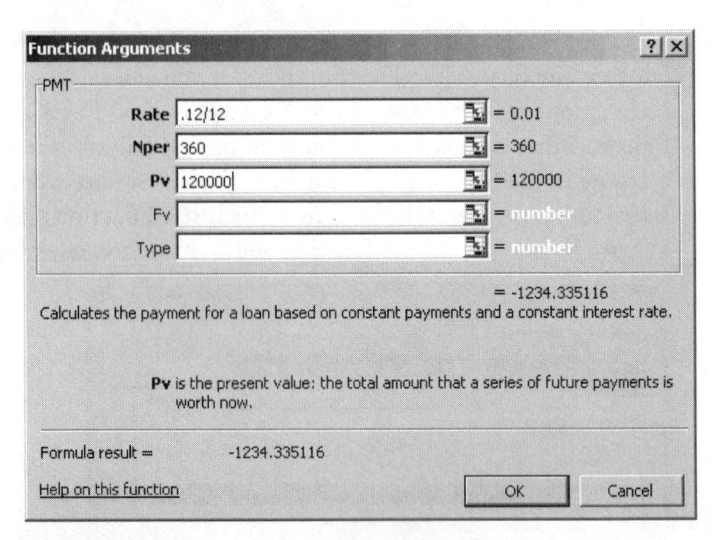

Figure F-17   Selecting data required for a function.

SEE ALSO *Formula Auditing, Formulas*

Goal Seek

The Tools→Goal Seek command determines which input value for a formula produces a specified formula result. Goal Seek, then, lets you quantify what needs to happen in order to achieve some specified result.

For example, suppose you want to determine the interest rate that would result in a $1,400-a-month payment on a $100,000 loan with a 10-year repayment term using the workbook (see Figure G-1).

Excel 2002 From A to Z

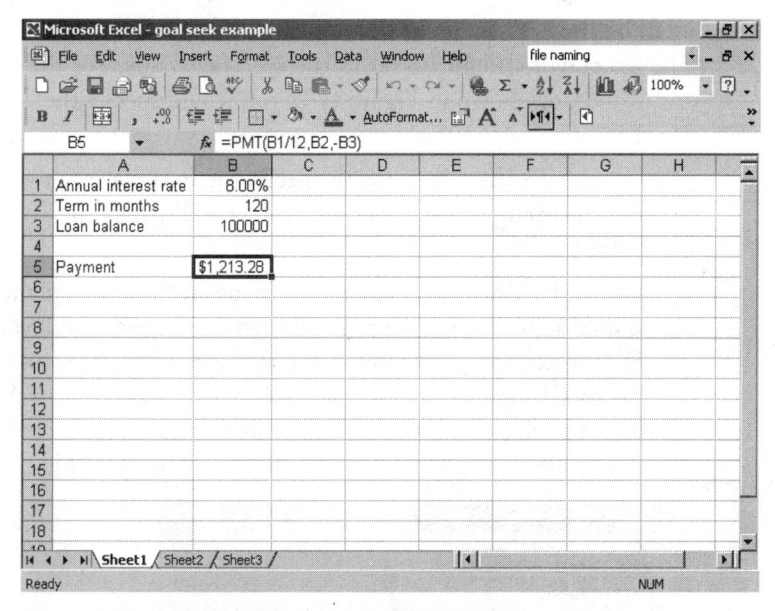

Figure G-1 A simple loan payment workbook.

NOTE   *In the loan payment workbook, cells B1, B2, and B3 hold loan payment function input values for the interest rate, the number of payments, and the loan amount. Cell B5 holds the formula =PMT(B1/12,B2,-B3) calculate the monthly interest payment.*

To determine the interest rate input value required for your specified formula result, follow these steps:

1. Choose the Tools→Goal Seek command. Excel displays the Goal Seek dialog box (see Figure G-2).

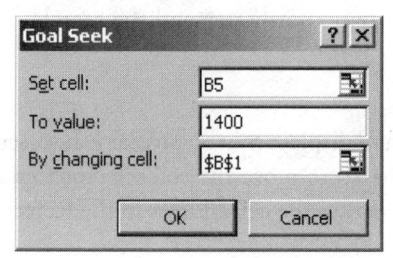

Figure G-2 The Goal Seek dialog box.

83

2. Use the Set Cell text box to specify the cell that holds the formula Excel will attempt to set to the specified value. For the example workbook shown in Figure G-2, you would specify the Set cell as B5.

3. Use the To Value text box to specify the formula result you want. For the example discussed here, you would specify the To Value as 1400.

4. Use the By Changing Cell text box to specify the input cell that Excel should adjust in an attempt to calculate the formula result you want. For the example workbook shown in Figure G-1, you would specify the By Changing cell to B1. When click OK, Excel adjusts the input cell to a value that produces the desired formula result and displays the results in the Goal Seek Status dialog box (see Figure G-3).

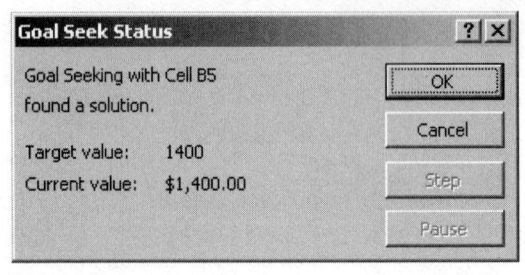

Figure G-3 The Goal Seek Status dialog box.

Goal Seek typically finds the correct input cell value in a fraction of a second. If your calculations are very cumbersome, however, Goal Seek may take longer. When this happens, you can click the Goal Seek Status dialog box's Stop button to terminate the search. Or you can click the Pause button to temporarily suspend the search.

Go To

The Edit→Go To command displays the Go To dialog box (see Figure G-4). You can use the Go To to move the cell selector to a new location in a workbook. Just enter the cell address in the Reference box and click OK.

Figure G-4   The Go To dialog box.

NOTE   *The Go To list in the Go To dialog box lists any cell and range names in your workbook. To go to one of these ranges, click the range and then OK.*

Graph see Charts

Graphic Objects see Pictures

Gridlines

Excel draws gridlines both on the worksheets you see in the workbook window and on the workbooks you print. You can remove these gridlines, however.

To print worksheets without gridlines, choose the File→Page Setup command, click the Sheet tab, and uncheck the Gridlines box (see Figure G-5).

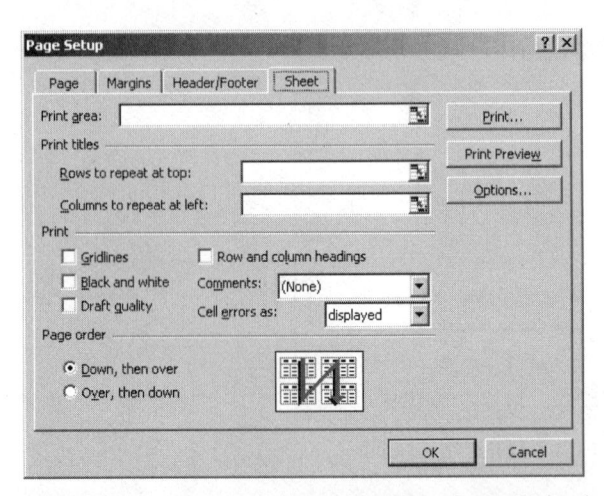

Figure G-5 The Sheet tab of the Page Setup dialog box.

To display worksheets in workbook windows without gridlines, choose the Tools→Options command, click the View tab, and uncheck the Gridlines box (see Figure G-6).

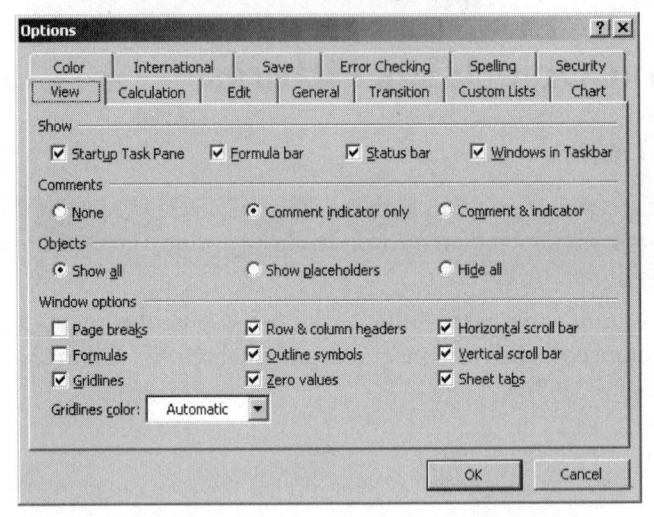

Figure G-6 The View tab of the Options dialog box.

Handwriting Recognition

To use the Handwriting Recognition tool built into Office XP programs, follow these steps:

Excel 2002 From A to Z

1. Display the Language toolbar by clicking on the EN indicator in the status area of the Window and choosing the Show Language Bar command.

   NOTE *The EN indicator doesn't appear in the status area until you turn on Office XP's speech recognition feature.*

2. Optionally, open the Writing Pad by clicking the Handwriting toolbar button and choose the Writing Pad command from the menu that the Language Bar displays. The Writing Pad window opens (see Figure H-1).

   NOTE *To write directly into the active workbook window, choose the Write Anywhere command from the Handwriting menu.*

Figure H-1   The Writing Pad window.

3. Place the cell selector or insertion point at the location where you want your text inserted. Then, using your mouse or handwriting input device, neatly write or print text inside the Writing Pad window. Don't pause as your write words. Do leave a space between words. As you write, Handwriting Recognition interprets your words, entering them at the insertion point. If you write something you want to erase, click the Writing Pad's Clear button.

   TIP *The Writing Pad window includes buttons you can click to represent common keys such as the Backspace, Spacebar, Enter and Tab keys. If you click the Expand button, The Writing Pad window expands to include buttons you can click to move the cursor one character up, down, right or left, to open the Drawing toolbar, and to display an onscreen keyboard you can use by clicking its buttons.*

4. To correct text you've entered with Handwriting Recognition, select the text and then either type the replacement text or handwrite the replacement text and click the Writing Pad's Correction button.

SEE ALSO *Drawing*

Headers and Footers

To create a header or footer for printed copies of a workbook, choose the View→Header and Footer command. Then select header or footer from the Header/Footer tab (see Figure H-2).

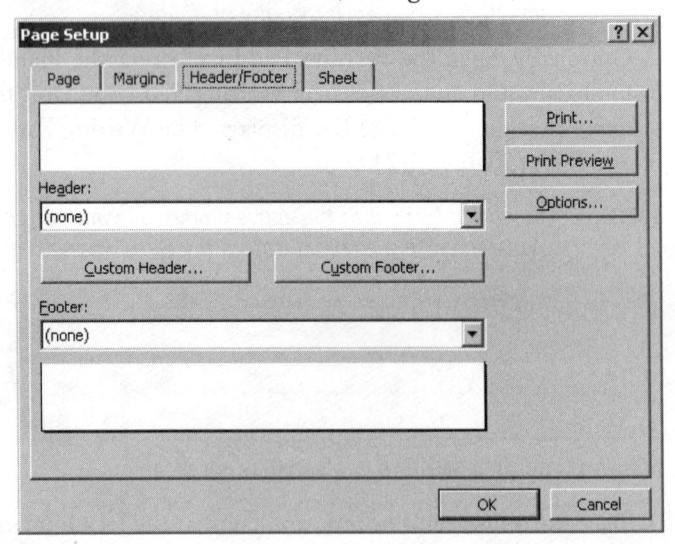

Figure H-2   The Header/Footer tab of the Page Setup dialog box.

NOTE   *You can use headers and footers to add information such as a page number, the company name, or the workbook name to printed copies of the workbook.*

Help see Office Assistant, Troubleshooting

Horizontal Page Orientation see Page Orientation

HTML

HTML is the file format used in Web pages. Excel will open and save HTML documents, which means you can use Excel to create Web pages. To create an HTML or Web page in Excel, follow these steps:

1. Choose the File→Save As command.

Excel 2002 From A to Z   H

2. Use the Save In and Filename to specify where the Web Page should be saved and what it should be named.
3. Select the Web Page entry from the Save File As Type box.
4. Click OK.

SEE ALSO *Web Folders*

Hyperlinks

Hyperlinks are clickable pictures and words you can use to display a network or Internet resource—such as a Web page. To use a hyperlink, you simply click it. Excel then opens the network resource (this might be another Excel workbook) or the Internet resource (probably a Web page).

Linking to an Existing File or Web Page

To create a hyperlink to another file or Web page, follow these steps:

1. Select the text or picture you want to turn into a hyperlink.
2. Choose the Insert→Hyperlink command. When Excel displays the Insert Hyperlink dialog box, click the Link To: Existing File Or Web Page button (see Figure H-3).

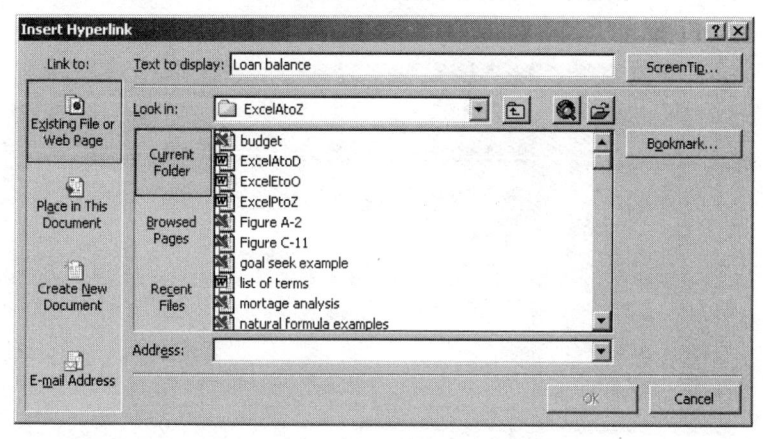

Figure H-3   The Insert Hyperlink dialog box with the Link To: Existing File Or Web Page options displayed.

3. Enter the Internet URL or network pathname that the hyperlink should point to in the Address box.

89

TIP   *If you don't know the URL or network pathname, you may be able to find the workbook or web page by clicking the Current Folder, Browsed Pages and Recent Files buttons and then choosing the workbook or web page from the list box. You can also use the Look In box and the Up One Folder button to display the contents of other folders on your local network and the Browse The Web button to open a web browser window you can use to find the page you want to link to.*

4. Use the Text To Display box to provide text the web browser should display in its status bar when someone points to the link.

5. Optionally, use the ScreenTip button to provide text the web browser will display in a pop-up box when someone points to the link.

Linking to a Place in the Open Workbook

To create a hyperlink to another location in the open workbook, follow these steps:

1. Select the text or picture you want to turn into a hyperlink.

2. Choose the Insert→Hyperlink command. When Excel displays the Insert Hyperlink dialog box, click the Place In This Document button (see Figure H-4).

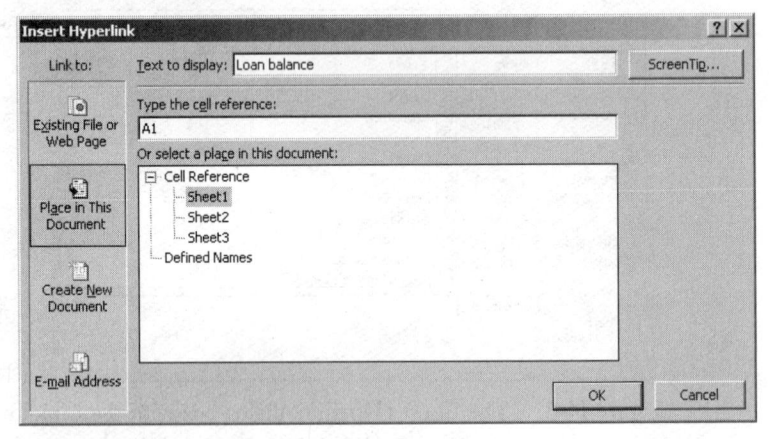

Figure H-4   The Insert Hyperlink dialog with the Place In This Document options displayed.

90

3. Use the Type The Cell Reference box or the Or Select A Place In This Document box to indicate where in the open document you want to link.

4. Use the Text To Display box to provide text the web browser should display in its status bar when someone points to the link.

5. Optionally, use the ScreenTip button to provide text the web browser will display in a pop-up box when someone points to the link.

Linking to a New Document

To create a hyperlink to a new document, follow these steps:

1. Select the text or picture you want to turn into a hyperlink.

2. Choose the Insert→Hyperlink command. When Excel displays the Insert Hyperlink dialog box, click the Create New Document button (see Figure H-5).

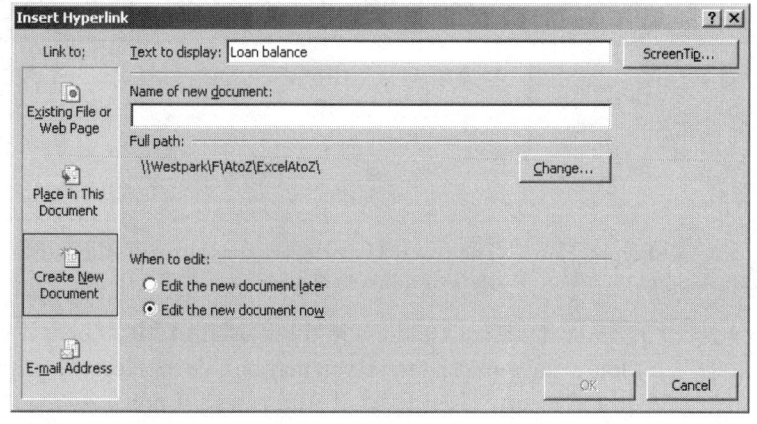

Figure H-5 The Insert Hyperlink dialog box with the Create New Document options displayed.

3. Enter the pathname of the new document in the Name Of New Document text box.

4. Use the Text To Display box to provide text the web browser should display in its status bar when someone points to the link.

5. Optionally, use the ScreenTip button to provide text the web browser will display in a pop-up box when someone points to the link.

6. To create the document now, click the Edit The New Document Now button. Or, to postpone creating the document, click the Edit The New Document Later button.

Linking to an E-Mail Address

To create a hyperlink to an e-mail address, follow these steps:

1. Select the text or picture you want to turn into a hyperlink.

2. Choose the Insert→Hyperlink command. When Excel displays the Insert Hyperlink dialog box, click the E-Mail Address button (see Figure H-6).

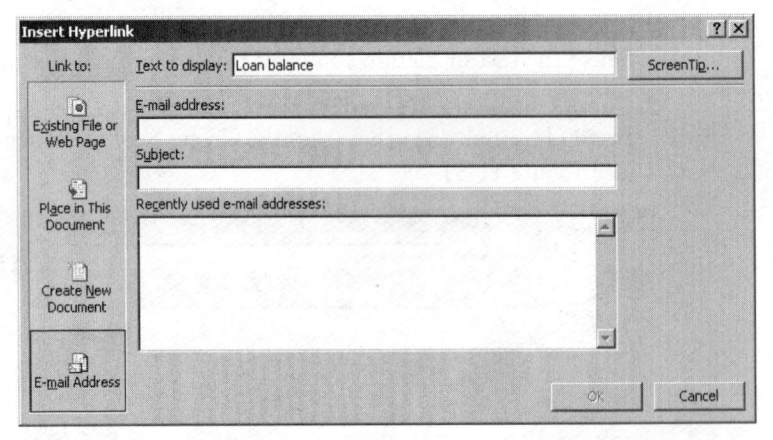

Figure H-6   The Insert Hyperlink dialog box with the E-Mail Address options displayed.

3. Enter the e-mail address in the E-Mail Address box. If you don't know the e-mail address, you may be able to select the address from the Recently Used E-Mail Addresses list box.

4. Optionally, enter a suggested message subject in the Subject box.

5. Use the Text To Display box to provide text the web browser should display in its status bar when someone points to the link.

6. Optionally, use the ScreenTip button to provide text the web browser will display in a pop-up box when someone points to the link.

Editing and Removing a Hyperlink

To change a hyperlink, right-click the hyperlink and choose the Edit Hyperlink command from the shortcut menu. Excel displays a dialog box like the one you originally used to create the hyperlink. Use it to make your changes.

To remove a hyperlink, right-click the hyperlink and choose the Remove Hyperlink command from the shortcut menu.

SEE ALSO *HTML, Web Pages*

Importing Databases

You may be able to import information from an external database and place that information in an Excel workbook. To import database information, you use the Data→Import External Data command. Excel starts the Data Connection Wizard, which steps you through the import process.

NOTE   *The first time you import data into Excel, you may need the assistance of the database administrator. You may also need a password.*

SEE ALSO *Text Files, Workbooks*

Indentation see Formatting Toolbar

Inserting Cell, Rows, Columns, and Worksheets

To insert a cell in a column or row, choose the Insert→Cells command. Excel displays the Insert dialog box (see Figure I-1). Click the Shift Cells Right button to insert a new cell in a row or click the Shift Cells Down button to insert a new cell in a column. After you've selected the appropriate option button, click OK.

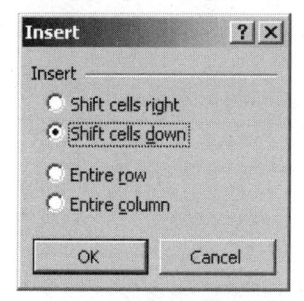

Figure I-1 The Insert dialog box.

To insert a row, click any cell in the row below where you want the new row inserted. Then choose the Insert→Rows command.

To insert a column, click any cell in the column to the right of where you want the new column inserted and choose the Insert→Columns command.

To insert a worksheet, display the worksheet in front of which you want to create a new worksheet and choose the Insert→Worksheet command.

SEE ALSO *Deleting Rows, Columns and Worksheets*

Insertion Point

The insertion point is the flashing vertical line that shows where what you type is placed in a cell. You can move the insertion by clicking the mouse (the insertion point moves to where you click) or by using the arrow keys (the insertion point moves one character in the direction of the arrow).

SEE ALSO *Editing Cell Contents*

Labels

Labels are simply any information entered in worksheet cells that you don't want to manipulate arithmetically. Labels often identify the values that are subject to calculation, so you normally enter them as the first stage in setting up a worksheet. Usually, labels are pieces of text that label input values and calculation results (see Figure L-1). However, they can also be numbers that won't be used arithmetically, such as telephone numbers or part or project ID numbers.

Excel 2002 From A to Z   L

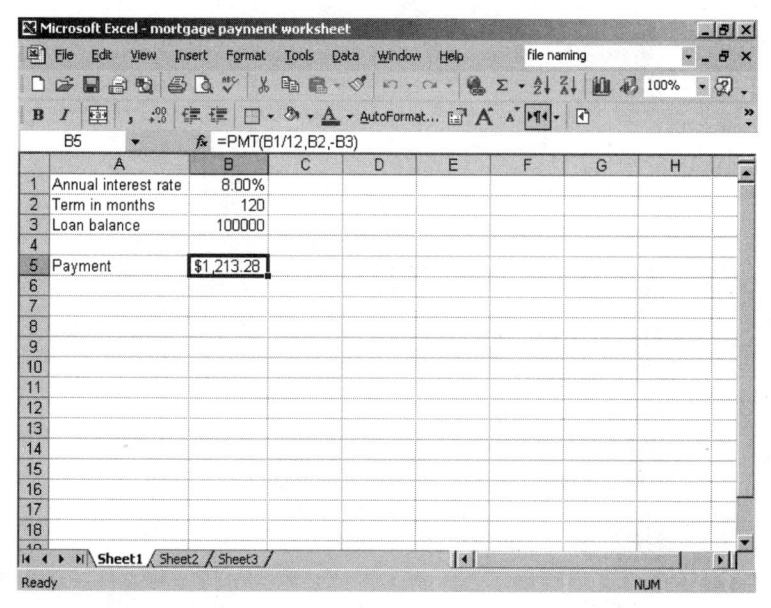

Figure L-1   A worksheet with labels in column A.

To enter a label, click the cell and then type the label. Set the label in the cell by pressing the Enter key, clicking the Enter button on the formula bar, or moving to another cell.

Landscape Orientation see Page Orientation

Linking Objects see Embedding Objects

Lists

An Excel list is a simple database that you can search, sort, and filter. Each row of the list, or database, holds a record, and each column holds a field. For example, if you have a database of employees, the various pieces of information about a single employee make up a record; the rows store this information about the individual employees. A piece of information, such as the employee's salary, is a field; the columns contain this same piece of information across all employees (see Figure L-2).

95

L | Excel 2002 From A to Z

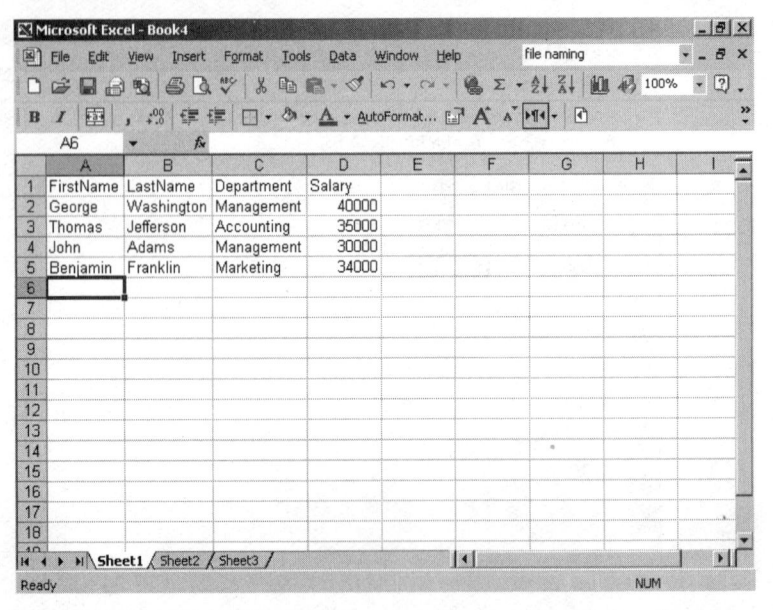

Figure L-2 A worksheet set up to hold an employee list, or database.

Creating a List

To create a list, follow these steps:

1. Open a new blank workbook.

2. Determine what each record should be. The information these records hold becomes the records' fields. For example, if you want to build a database of employees, each employee's information goes into a separate record.

3. Enter the field labels in the first row of the worksheet (see Figure L-2).

4. To add information to your list, you can click a cell and type the label or value the field should hold.

You can also enter records into your list by selecting the header row, choosing the Data→Form command, clicking OK, and then entering records using the data form dialog box (see Figure L-3). If the form field boxes are not blank, click New to create a New record. But then fill in the information about the first record by entering data in the appropriate boxes. Click New to add the new record to the worksheet and display a new blank form. Excel adds a new row to the worksheet for the new record. When you're finished using a form to enter records, click Close.

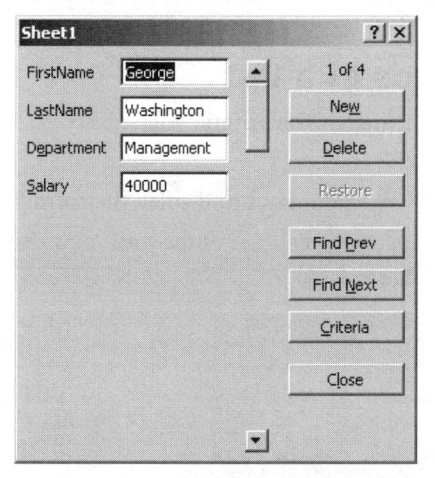

Figure L-3 The data form dialog box Excel creates to enter records into the worksheet shown in Figure L-2.

Editing List Records

You can edit records by changing the contents of the cells that hold the list information.

You can also redisplay the form and use it to edit records. To edit records using a form, follow these steps:

1. Choose the Data→Form command to redisplay the form.
2. Click Find Prev to page backward through the records one by one, or click Find Next to page forward through the records one by one. You can also use the scroll bar to scroll through the database to the record you want to edit.
3. Enter your changes in the form's fields. If you make a mistake when editing a form, click Restore to undo all of your changes to the record.

NOTE   *To delete a record, click Delete. Excel deletes this row from the worksheet.*

4. Update the worksheet with your changes to the record. Click Find Next or Find Prev to edit other records, click New to add a new record, or click Close to return to the worksheet.

Finding Records in a List

To use find records that match the criteria you specify, follow these steps:

1. Choose the Data→Form command to display the form.
2. Click Criteria. The upper right corner of the form now displays the word *Criteria* (see Figure L-4).

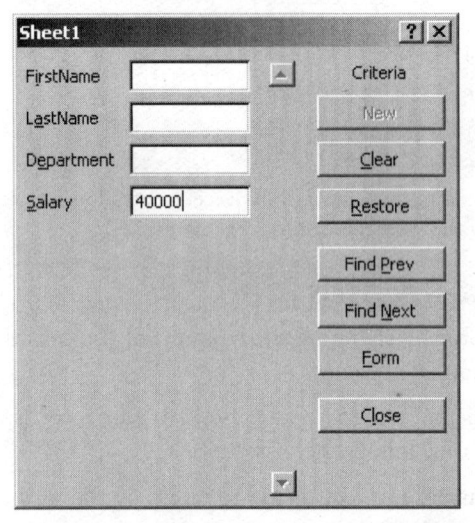

Figure L-4   Finding a record in a database.

3. Enter the search criteria in the form's fields.
4. Click Find Prev or Find Next. Excel finds the previous or next record matching the criteria you specified.

NOTE   *You can also use the Edit→Find command to find items in a list.*

Sorting a List

To sort a list, follow these steps:

1. Click a cell in the database. Doing so tells Excel that you want to sort all the fields in the database and keep the records intact.

Excel 2002 From A to Z

WARNING *If you select a range that doesn't include all columns, Excel orts the columns in your range but does not sort the other columns in the database. This disassociates fields from the records to which they belong and attaches them to other records.*

TIP *To sort only a part of a database, select all rows for the records you want to sort.*

2. Choose the Data→Sort command. Excel displays the Sort dialog box shown in Figure L-5.

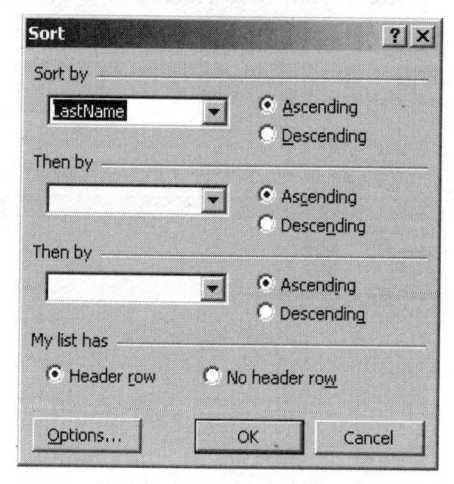

Figure L-5 The Sort dialog box.

3. Use the Sort By drop-down list box to select the name of the field by which you want to sort the database.

4. Click the Ascending option button to sort with the lowest number, first letter of the alphabet, or earliest date at the top of the column. Click the Descending option button to sort in reverse numeric, alphabetic, or chronological order.

NOTE *Regardless of whether you click Ascending or Descending, blank fields appear at the bottom of the list.*

5. If multiple entries in the field you're sorting by are the same, you can specify other fields by which you want to sort using the Then By drop-down list boxes and corresponding Ascending and Descending option buttons.

6. Select the Header Row option button. If you don't, Excel sorts your field labels along with the data in the fields.
7. Click OK.

Filtering Lists

To filter a database, follow these steps:

1. Select a cell in the database.
2. Choose the Data→Filter→AutoFilter command. Excel adds arrow buttons to the right side of your field labels in the first row (see Figure L-6).

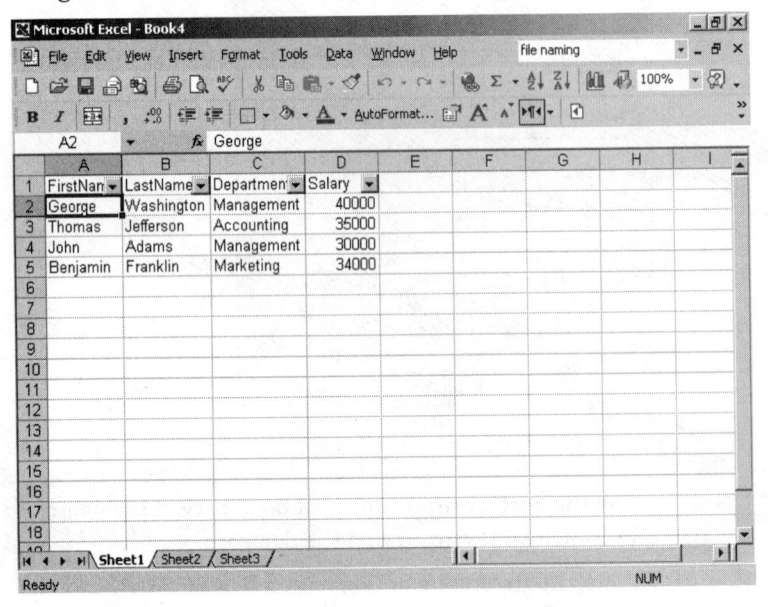

Figure L-6   Filtering field entries.

3. Click the arrow for the field by which you want to filter records.

Excel displays a drop-down list of the entries in that field.

- If you want to include only a single entry, select the entry from the list.
- To display only a given top or bottom percent or number of entries, select Top 10 from the list. Excel displays the Top 10 AutoFilter dialog box (see Figure L-7). Use it to specify whether you want to

view the top or bottom entries in the field and the number or percentage of entries you want to view. Click OK when you're finished.

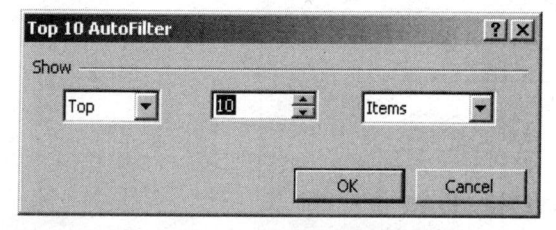

Figure L-7   The Top 10 AutoFilter dialog box.

- To customize the filter, choose Custom from the list. Excel displays the Custom AutoFilter dialog box (see Figure L-8). Use the first drop-down list box to select the operator. Use the second drop-down list box to enter the text or value on which you're basing the filter. Optionally, click the And or Or option button to specify another criteria and use the second row of drop-down list boxes to describe the second criteria. Click OK when you're finished.

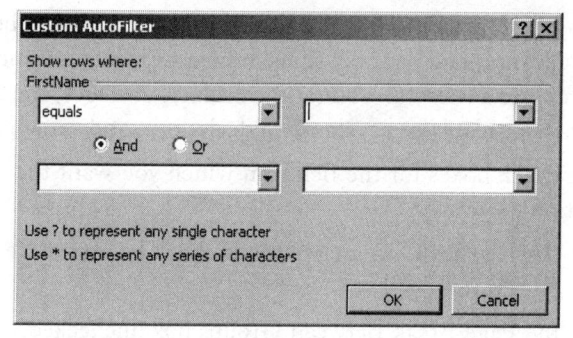

Figure L-8   The Custom AutoFilter dialog box.

Subtotaling Lists

To subtotal information in a list, follow these steps:

1. Select a cell in the database, and choose the Data→Subtotals command. Excel displays the Subtotal dialog box (see Figure L-9).

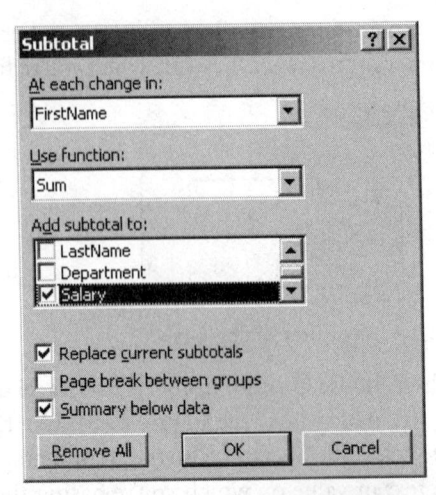

Figure L-9 The Subtotal dialog box.

2. Use the At Each Change In drop-down list box to specify the field by which you want the subtotals grouped.

3. Select a function from the Use Function drop-down list box. The Subtotal command not only sums—the usual function since that's how you get a subtotal—but also calculates averages, the number of entries or blank items, standard deviations, and variances.

4. Select check boxes for the fields on which you want the subtotal operation performed.

5. Select the Replace Current Subtotals check box if you've created subtotals before.

6. Leave the Page Break Between Groups box unchecked.

7. Select the Summary Below Data check box unless you want the subtotals to appear above rather than below the data they summarize.

8. Click OK. Excel adds subtotal and grand total rows to the database. To remove subtotals, choose the Data→Subtotals command and click Remove All in the Subtotal dialog box.

TIP — *You can hide and display subtotal groups by clicking the boxes with the plus and minus signs in the outline area on the left. You can also click the numbers at the top of the outline area to view specific levels of the outline.*

Validating List Entries

Excel can validate new records, thereby ensuring that they fit certain criteria. This can help prevent someone from entering, for example, a label (like a name) into a field that should hold a value (such as the person's salary).

To set up validation criteria, follow these steps:

1. Select the range of cells to which you want the criteria to apply.

2. Choose the Data→Validation command and click the Settings tab. Excel displays the Data Validation dialog box (see Figure L-10).

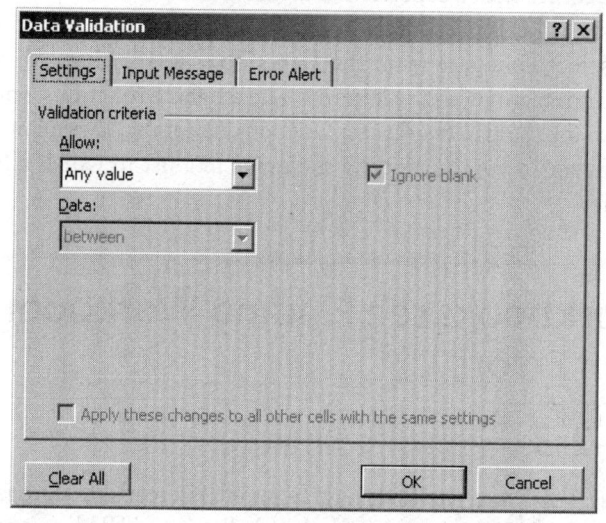

Figure L-10 The Settings tab of the Data Validation dialog box.

3. Select a type of data from the Allow drop-down list box. After you select a data type, Excel displays other boxes, which allow you to constrain the type of data you selected. For example, if you selected Date, Excel prompts you to select the start- and end-date boundaries.

4. Click the Input Message tab, and create a prompt to inform database users which input is allowable. Optionally, enter a short title for the message in the Title box. Enter the message text in the Input Message box. If you enter records directly in the database and do not use a form, Excel displays the input message when you select a cell to which the validation criteria applies.

5. Click the Error Alert tab to customize the pop-up error message that will appear if a person enters invalid data. Select a symbol from the Style drop-down list box. Optionally, enter a title for the message in the Title box. Enter the message text in the Error Message box.

NOTE *The validation rules apply whether you enter data directly into the database worksheet or use a form.*

Using Database Functions

Excel comes with a collection of database functions tailored especially for lists. To see these functions, choose the Insert→Function command and select Database from the Function Category list. All of these functions begin with the letter D. The database functions work similarly to the standard worksheet functions except that they allow an extra parameter so you can specify the items in a list to which a function applies.

Lost Workbooks see Finding Workbooks, Program Errors

Lotus 1-2-3

Lotus 1-2-3 was the first, hugely popular spreadsheet program and in the early 1980s almost single-handedly turned IBM's new personal computer into a must-have tool for businesses.

Many spreadsheet files still use the once-popular Lotus 1-2-3 file format, and Microsoft Excel easily saves and opens Lotus 1-2-3 worksheets.

SEE ALSO *Workbooks*

Macros

Macros are sequences of keystrokes or commands. You use macros within Excel to automate repetitive actions.

Creating a Macro

To create a macro, follow these steps:

1. Choose the Tools→Macro→Record New Macro command. Excel displays the Record Macro dialog box (see Figure M-1).

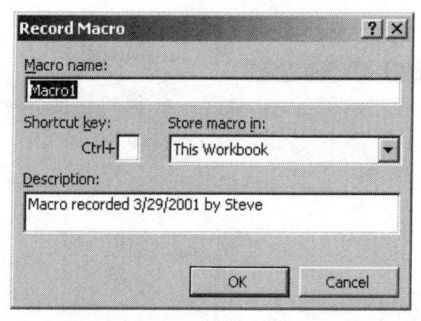

Figure M-1 The Record Macro dialog box.

2. Enter a name for the macro into the Macro Name box. You can use up to 80 characters but no spaces or symbols for the name.

3. Indicate whether you'll run the macro by using the Toolbars button or by using the Keyboard button:

   - Click the Toolbars button to create a toolbar button for the macro. When Excel displays the Toolbars tab of the Customize dialog box, click the Commands tab and then the Macros entry in the Categories list. Then, drag the new macro—Excel will show it in the Commands list—to the toolbar.

   - Click the Keyboard button to create a keyboard shortcut for the macro. When Excel displays the Customize Keyboard dialog box, click the Press New Shortcut Key, press the key combination you want to use to run the macro, and then click Assign.

4. Type the keystrokes and choose the commands that you want your macro to run and choose.

5. Choose the Tools→Macros→Stop Recording command.

Running a Macro

You can run the macros you create in three ways:

- You can click the macro's toolbar button.
- You can press the macro's key combination.

M Excel 2002 From A to Z

- You can choose the Tools→Macro→Macros command to display the Macro dialog box and then double-click the macro you want to run (see Figure M-2).

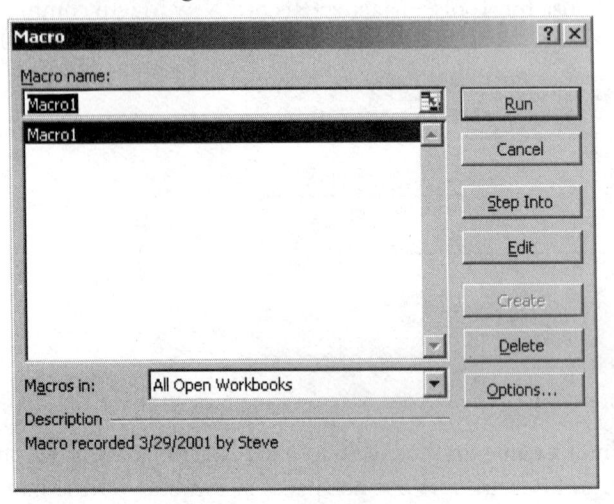

Figure M-2 The Macro dialog box.

NOTE *Editing and debugging Excel macros, which are written in the Visual Basic for Applications programming language, is beyond the scope of this book. If you're interested in Visual Basic programming and you haven't programmed before, you'll find it useful to have a book that describes and discusses Visual Basic.*

Macro Security

To adjust Excel's macro security, choose the Tools→Options command, click the Security tab, and then click the Macro Security button. Excel displays the Security dialog box (see Figure M-3). Use the Security Level tab's buttons to tell Excel which macros it can safely run. Use the Trusted Sources tab to list the macro authors you've said you trust or to remove a macro author from a trusted source.

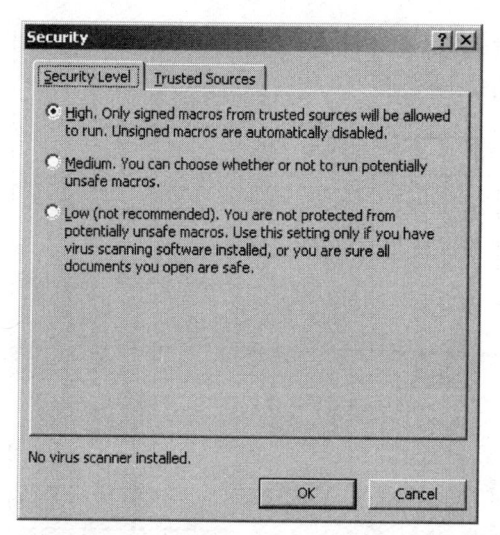

Figure M-3 The Security Level tab of the Security dialog box.

SEE ALSO *Password Protecting a Workbook, Privacy Options*

Magnification see Zoom

Manual Recalculation see Recalculation

Margin

To set the page margins for printed copies of your workbook, choose the File→Page Setup command and click the Margins tab (see Figure M-4). Use the Margin boxes, Top, Left, Bottom and Right to specify how large a margin should appear around the workbook's text.

M Excel 2002 From A to Z

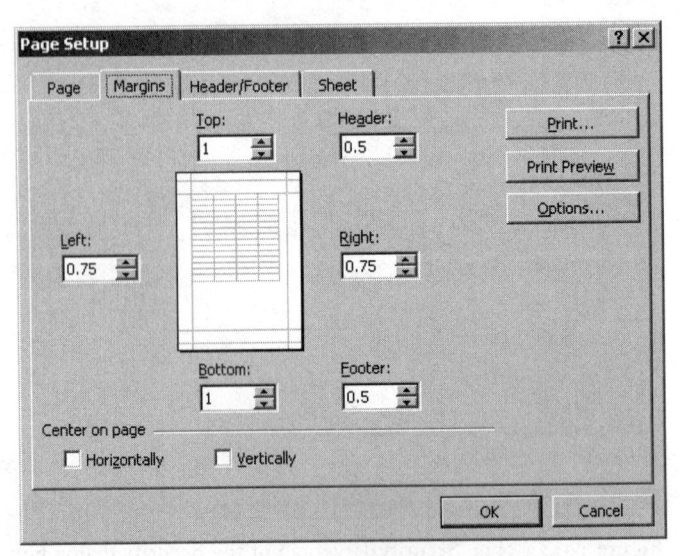

Figure M-4 The Margins tab of the Page Setup dialog box.

TIP   Check the Horizontally and Vertically boxes to center your printed workbook's information on its pages.

Microsoft Office User Specialist

Microsoft certifies Excel users who can pass a test as Microsoft Office User Specialists, and in the parlance of Microsoft, these people then become MOUS certified. You don't learn anything new by becoming a MOUS certificate holder, but if you're in a career or an organization where certification delivers benefits, know that these tests are relatively straight-forward to prepare and pass.

Your first step is to learn what material you need to know to pass the test you want to take. You can get a summary of the material tested from Microsoft's Web site at www.microsoft.com. Just visit the web site and search on the term:

```
Microsoft Office User Specialist (MOUS) Excel 2002
Exam Objectives
```

After you know what you need to know in order to pass the test, practice every task or skill a few times. You don't need a special study test or a class. This book should tell you everything you need to know.

108

After you've prepared, take the test at a local testing center. You can learn about any local testing centers from the local telephone directory or from the Microsoft Web site.

TIP *Perhaps the most important skill for passing a MOUS test is knowing how to use the Office Assistant. You can't rely on this tool to answer every question the test asks—there isn't time—but as long as you're comfortable using the Office Assistant, you should have time to ask it the question or two you can't answer on your own.*

SEE ALSO Office Assistant

Mixed Cell Addresses see Copying Formulas

Moving Cell Contents

Excel provides several ways to move text:

- **Drag-and-drop.** Select text you want to move by dragging the mouse. Then drag the selected text to a new location.

- **Edit→Cut and Edit→Paste commands.** Select the cell, range or text, choose the Edit→Cut command, position the cell selector or insertion point at the new location, and choose the Edit→Paste command.

- **Cut and Paste toolbar buttons.** Select the cell, range or text, click the Cut button, position the cell selector or insertion point at the new location, and choose the Paste toolbar button.

- **Office Clipboard task pane.** Select the cell, range or text, click the Cut button or choose the Edit→Cut command, position the cell selector or insertion point at the new location, and click the item you want to paste from the Office Clipboard. (If the Office Clipboard doesn't show, choose the Edit→Office Clipboard command.)

NOTE *When you move a formula, Excel doesn't adjust the relative references used in the moved formula.*

NOTE   You aren't limited to moving ranges and text just within a workbook. You can move text between Excel workbooks and between different program's workbooks—such as from your e-mail program to Excel. The only trick is that after you cut the text, you need to open the workbook into which you want to paste the text before positioning the insertion point. When you move a range, the range may appear as a table in the document it's pasted into.

SEE ALSO *Clipboard, Copying Cell Contents*

Moving Objects

To move the selected object, such as a picture, click the Cut toolbar button, position the cell selector or insertion point at the location where the object should be moved, and click the Paste toolbar button.

Moving Around a Workbook

With three (or more) sheets, 256 columns, and 65,536 rows, an Excel workbook is so large that only a small area is visible on screen at one time. Not surprisingly, Excel provides several ways for you to view different portions of the workbook displayed in the program window:

- With the mouse, you can use the vertical and horizontal scroll bars along the right and bottom edges of the workbook window to move through your worksheet. Just click inside the scroll bars to move one screen at a time. Click the scroll bar arrows to move one row or column.
- With the mouse, click a sheet tab to move to that worksheet or chart sheet in the workbook.
- Press Page Up and Page Down to scroll through the current worksheet one screen at a time. Hold down the Ctrl key and press Page Up or Page Down to the next or previous worksheet.
- The arrow keys move up and down, right and left one cell at a time. You can also move to the right one cell by pressing the Tab key and to the left one cell by holding down the Shift key while pressing Tab.
- To move directly to a specific cell, you can enter that cell's name in the Name box and press the Enter key. (The Name box is located at the left end of the formula bar.) You can also choose the Edit→Go To command, enter a cell reference in its Reference text box, and then click OK to move to the cell.

Naming Cells and Ranges

In the real world, Excel worksheets can be complex, and remembering, for example, that cell B1 contains the advertising expenses, that cell B2 contains the bank charges and so on, becomes difficult (see Figure N-1).

	A	B	C
1	Advertising	5000	
2	Bank Charges	500	
3	Car	6000	
4	Depreciation	1500	
5	Equipment	2000	
6	Total	15000	

Figure N-1   A sample worksheet that should use names.

Fortunately, Excel allows you to name cells and ranges and then use those names in your formulas. Instead of referring to cell B1 in a formula, you can refer to *Advertising* if you first name cell B1 *Advertising*. And if you name cells B1, B2, B3, B4, and B5 *Advertising, Bank, Car, Depreciation,* and *Equipment*, respectively, the following two formulas would be identical:

```
=B1+B2+B3+B4+B5
```

```
=Advertising+Bank+Car+Depreciation+Equipment
```

To name a cell, select the cell and then type the name into the name box. The Name box appears just above cell A1 and shows either the name of the active cell or its cell address (see Figure N-2).

	A	B	C
1	Advertising	5000	
2	Bank Charges	500	
3	Car	6000	
4	Depreciation	1500	
5	Equipment	2000	
6	Total	15000	

Figure N-2   A worksheet that uses cell names.

Range names must begin with a letter, not a number. They cannot include spaces, and they shouldn't look like cell references or function names.

Range names are useful in formulas and functions, but that's not their only use. Once you name a range, you can use the name in place of the range definition whenever Excel asks you for a range. For example, if you use the Go To command, you could enter a name instead of a cell address.

> **NOTE** *The Insert→Name command displays a submenu of commands useful for creating cell and range names too. For example, if you select the range A1:B5 in the worksheet shown in Figure N-1 and choose the Insert→Name→Create command, Excel will correctly name cells B1, B2, B3, B4, and B5 for you.*

#NAME Message see Error Messages

#N/A Message see Error Messages

Natural Language Formulas see Formulas

#NULL Message see Error Messages

Number Pages see Page Numbers

Numbers see Values

Office Assistant

In Office programs, the Office Assistant supplies help. To use the Office Assistant, click the Office Assistant. (If the Office Assistant isn't already displayed, choose the Help→Show Office Assistant command.) Then type your question into the box provided and click Search (see Figure O-1). The Office Assistant displays a list of help topics that may answer your question.

Excel 2002 From A to Z

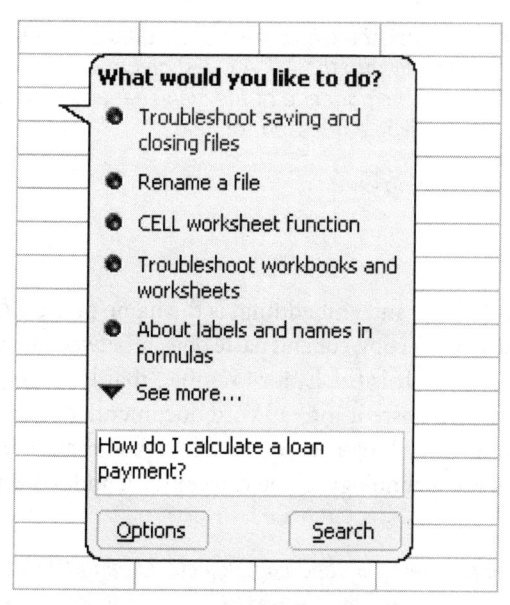

O

Figure O-1 The Office Assistant.

Click the help topic you want to see. The Office Assistant opens the Excel help file (see Figure O-2).

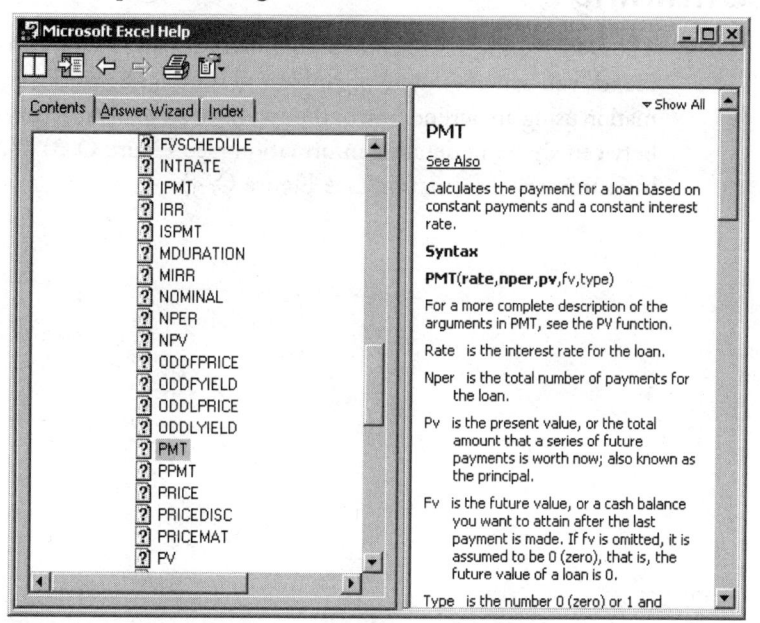

Figure O-2 The Help window.

113

TIP   You can also ask the Office Assistant a question by typing the question directly into the Ask A Question box. The Ask A Question box is on the right end of the menu bar and initially shows the phrase, "Type a question for help."

SEE ALSO *Troubleshooting*

OLE

OLE, or object linking and embedding, is the name of the Windows technology that lets you copy, cut and paste objects between workbooks and other documents. It is OLE, for example, that lets you copy an Excel chart and then paste it into a Word document. You don't have to know anything special in order to use OLE. And that's part of the attractiveness of the technology. If you can copy, cut and paste, you can use OLE.

SEE ALSO *Copying Objects, Embedding Objects, Moving Objects*

Optimization Modeling see Solver

Outlining

The Data→Group And Outline command displays a submenu of commands you can employ to organize and summarize worksheet information using an outline. You outline worksheets to make it easy to jump between showing detailed information (see Figure O-3) and showing summary information (see Figure O-4).

Excel 2002 From A to Z

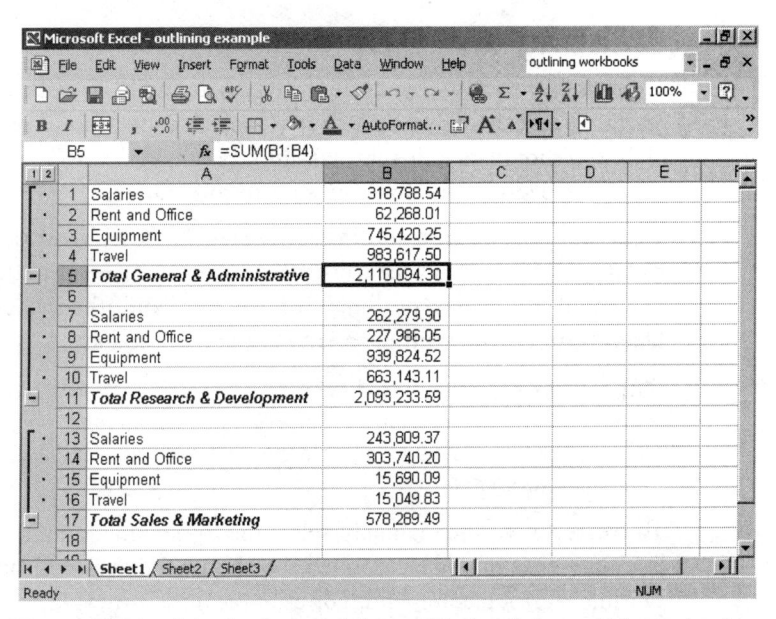

Figure O-3 A budgeting worksheet with detailed cost information by department.

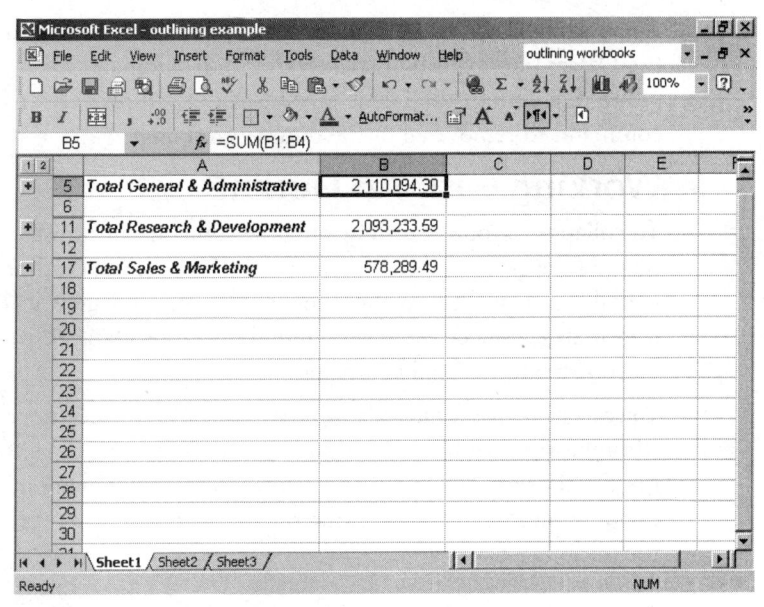

Figure O-4 A budgeting worksheet with only summary cost information by department.

115

Creating an Outline

To create an outline, your first step is to build a worksheet or rearrange an existing worksheet so it looks like one shown in Figure O-3. You should include subtotals information in the last row of each set of detailed information you want to summarize.

To create your outline automatically—and this won't work unless Excel can understand your worksheet organization—select the rows that hold the to-be-outlined information and then chose the Data→Group And Outline→Auto Outline command.

> **NOTE** *To determine how Excel outlines a worksheet, choose the Data→Group And Outline→Settings command. Then, use the Settings dialog box to describe how you've organized your worksheet.*

To create an outline manually, select the rows—including the heading row—that should be grouped and choose the Data→Group And Outline→Group command. For example, in Figure O-3, you could select rows 1 through 5 and choose the Group command to group the general and administrative expenses.

If you make a mistake in grouping, select the group and then choose the Data→Group And Outline→Ungroup command to remove the group. Or, choose the Data→Group And Outline→Clear Outline command to remove all of the outline groupings.

Working with An Outline

To collapse a group and show only the summary information, select a row of the group and choose the Data→Group And Outline→Hide Detail command. To expand a collapsed group and show its detailed information, select the group and choose the Data→Group And Outline→Show Detail command.

You can also expand and collapse groups by clicking the buttons marked with plus sign symbols and minus sign symbols along the left edge of the Excel program window. And you can control which outline levels, or groups, appear by clicking the numbered buttons at the top of the outlining pane.

Page Breaks

Excel automatically breaks workbooks into pages when you print. You can see where Excel breaks pages by print previewing. To do this, click the Print Preview button. If you don't want to use Excel's automatic page breaks, you can insert your own manual page breaks. To insert a manual page break click the cell that shows where the break should be, and then choose the Insert→Page Break command. To remove a manual page, click the cell that shows where the break is and choose the Insert→Remove Break command.

SEE ALSO *Workbooks*

Page Numbers

To insert page numbers in your workbook, add a header or footer that includes the page number.

SEE ALSO *Headers and Footers*

Page Orientation

Excel will print your pages in either a portrait orientation or a landscape orientation. To change the current orientation of the open workbook, choose the File→Page Setup command, click the Page tab, and then click either the Portrait or Landscape buttons (see Figure P-1).

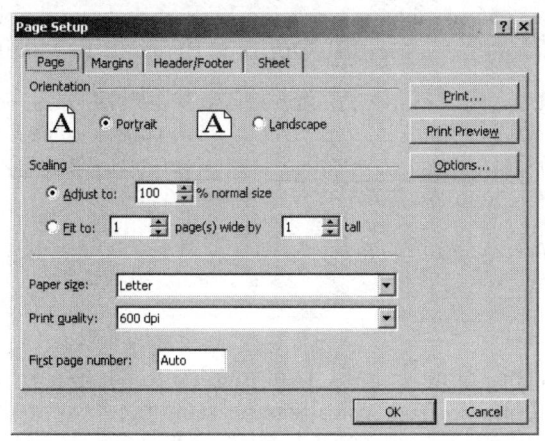

Figure P-1   The Page tab of the Page Setup dialog box.

Password Protecting a Workbook

To add password protection to a workbook, choose the File→Save As command, click the Tools button, and then choose the General Options command. Excel displays the Save Options dialog box, which you use to add and remove passwords (see Figure P-2).

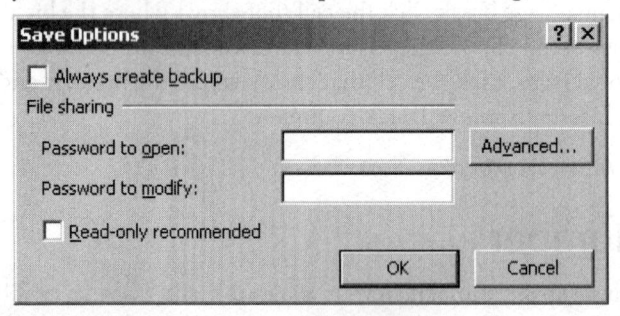

Figure P-2   The Save Options dialog box.

To add a password which Excel should require before it opens the workbook, enter the password into the Password To Open box. To add a password which Excel should require before it saves the workbook using the same name and location, enter the password into the Password To Modify box. Your passwords may use any combination of letters, symbols and numbers, up to 15 characters. Note that capitalization counts.

To remove a password from a previously protected workbook, delete the contents of the Password To Open and Password To Modify boxes.

> **NOTE**   *Click the Advanced button to display a list of encryption methods Excel can use to protect your workbook. While Excel's normal encryption is adequate in most settings, extremely sensitive data may warrant a more secure encryption.*

SEE ALSO *Macro Security, Privacy Options*

Pasting

When you copy or move some item, your last step is to paste the item from the clipboard. You typically paste using the Paste toolbar button, the Edit→Paste command, the Office Clipboard or, indirectly, by dragging the mouse.

SEE ALSO *Clipboard, Copying Cell Contents, Moving Cell Contents*

Paste Function see Functions

Paste Options Button

When you copy or cut and then paste a selection, Excel displays a Paste Options button in your workbook. This button, which looks like the toolbar's Paste button, displays a list of pasting options you can use to tell Excel if it should adjust the pasted selection:

- The Keep Source Formatting option tells Excel to use the same formatting for the pasted selection as the copied or cut selection uses.
- The Match Destination Formatting option tells Excel to format the pasted selection so that it matches the range into which it's been pasted.
- The Value And Number Formatting option tells Excel to use only the numeric formatting of the pasted selection but not other formatting (such as boldfacing or italics).
- The Keep Source Column Widths option tells Excel to use the same column widths in the range with the new pasted selection.
- The Formatting Only option tells Excel to paste only the formatting and not the labels, values or formulas.
- The Link Cells option tells Excel to link the pasted selection to the copied selection.

SEE ALSO *Clipboard, Copying Cell Contents*

Paste Special Dialog Box

If you want to specify pasting options, instead of just clicking the Paste button after copying or cutting, choose the Edit→Paste Special command. Excel displays the Paste Special dialog box (see Figure P-3). To paste a row of cells as a column of cells or vice versa, check the Transpose box. To paste only a portion of the copied or cut cells' contents, click a Paste option button other than All. For example, to paste only the comments, click the Comments option button under Paste. To add, subtract, multiply, or divide the values in the copied range with the values in the destination range, click the Add, Subtract, Multiply, or Divide option button under Operation. To tell Excel it shouldn't paste blank cells over values, check the Skip Blanks box.

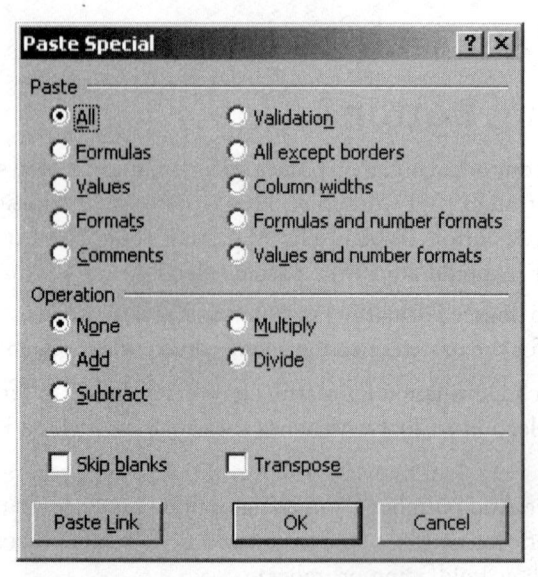

Figure P-3   The Paste Special dialog box.

Pathname

A pathname describes a file's location on your computer or network. Typically, a pathname includes three pieces, the disk or network drive letter, folder and subfolder information, and the file name and extension. For example, in the pathname

f:\atoz\excel\excelatoz.doc

the first portion of this pathname, *f:*, identifies the drive on which the folders and their files are stored. The second part of the pathname, *\atoz\excel*, names the folder and subfolder where the file is stored. The *atoz* part of the pathname identifies the folder, and the *excel* part of the pathname identifies the subfolder. The *excelatoz.doc* identifies the exact file by giving its file name and the file extension.

> NOTE   *The backslashes separate the drive letter, folder and subfolder names, and the workbook name.*

Personalized Menus and Toolbars

By default, Excel personalizes your menus and toolbars. Menu commands and toolbar buttons you're likely to use or that you've recently used appear. Menu commands and toolbar buttons that you're not likely to use or haven't used in a long time don't appear.

If you don't want to use or want to change the way the Excel's personalized menus and toolbars work, choose the Tools→Customize command and click Options tab (see Figure P-4). Use the Options tab to change the way the Excel's personalized menus and toolbars work.

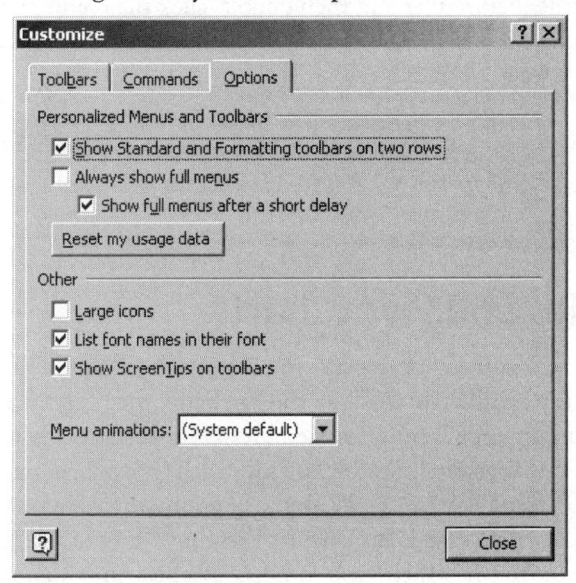

Figure P-4 The Options tab of the Customize dialog box.

- Check the Show Standard And Formatting Toolbars On Two Rows box to tell Excel to use two separate toolbars for the Standard and Formatting toolbars rather than one, personalized toolbar of just your most recently used tools.
- Check the Always Show Full Menus box to tell Excel to display full menus rather than personalized menus.
- Check the Show Full Menus After A Short Delay box if you're using personalized menus but want the full menu to appear if you hold the menu open for a few seconds.

- Click the Reset My Usage Data button to tell Excel to start over in its analysis of which commands you've recently or are frequently using. This analysis is what Excel uses to determine which commands and toolbar buttons go onto your personalized menus and toolbars.

Pictures

You can add pictures to your Excel workbooks by choosing the Insert→Picture→From File command. When Excel displays the Insert Picture dialog box, use the Look In box to select the folder containing the picture files and then double-click the picture image you want to insert.

> **NOTE** *You can copy and move pictures in the same way that you copy and move other objects in a workbook. You resize a picture object by clicking the picture to select it and then dragging the selection handles. To delete a picture, click it and press Delete.*

SEE ALSO *Clip Art*

PivotTables and PivotCharts

If you use Excel to list records, you can use the PivotTables feature to sort, filter, and pivot fields so you can better focus on the information you want. For example, a microbrewery that sells six types of beer on the West coast might record sales for each type of beer by state and by season (see Figure P-5). With the large amount of information in the list, spotting trends is difficult. Creating a PivotTable, however, allows you to see which type of beer sells best in which region or during which season.

Excel 2002 FROM A TO Z   P

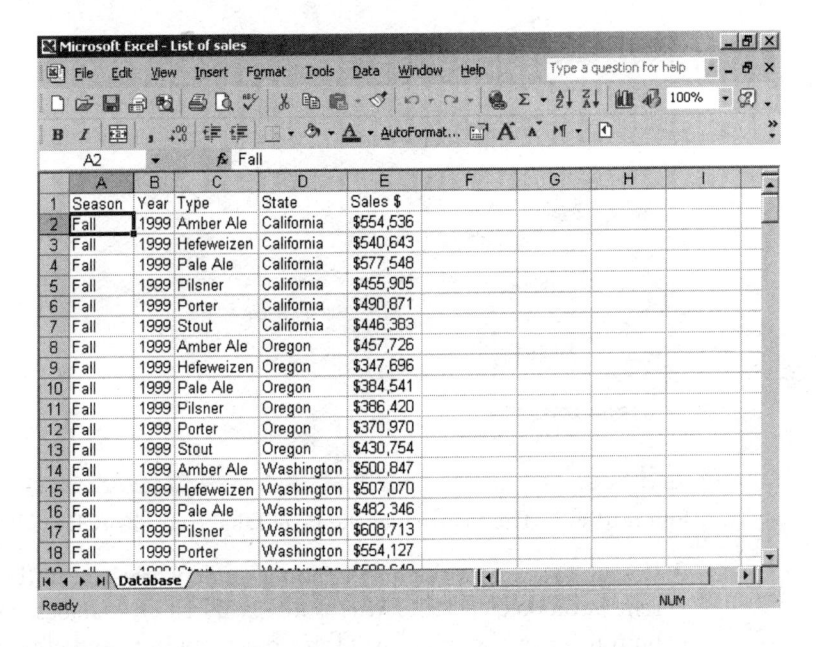

	A	B	C	D	E
1	Season	Year	Type	State	Sales $
2	Fall	1999	Amber Ale	California	$554,536
3	Fall	1999	Hefeweizen	California	$540,643
4	Fall	1999	Pale Ale	California	$577,548
5	Fall	1999	Pilsner	California	$455,905
6	Fall	1999	Porter	California	$490,871
7	Fall	1999	Stout	California	$446,383
8	Fall	1999	Amber Ale	Oregon	$457,726
9	Fall	1999	Hefeweizen	Oregon	$347,696
10	Fall	1999	Pale Ale	Oregon	$384,541
11	Fall	1999	Pilsner	Oregon	$386,420
12	Fall	1999	Porter	Oregon	$370,970
13	Fall	1999	Stout	Oregon	$430,754
14	Fall	1999	Amber Ale	Washington	$500,847
15	Fall	1999	Hefeweizen	Washington	$507,070
16	Fall	1999	Pale Ale	Washington	$482,346
17	Fall	1999	Pilsner	Washington	$608,713
18	Fall	1999	Porter	Washington	$554,127

Figure P-5   Excel list of beer sales.

Using the PivotTable Wizard

To use the PivotTable Wizard, follow these steps:

1. Select any cell in the database and choose the Data→PivotTable And PivotChart Report command. Excel starts the PivotTable And PivotChart Wizard (see Figure P-6).

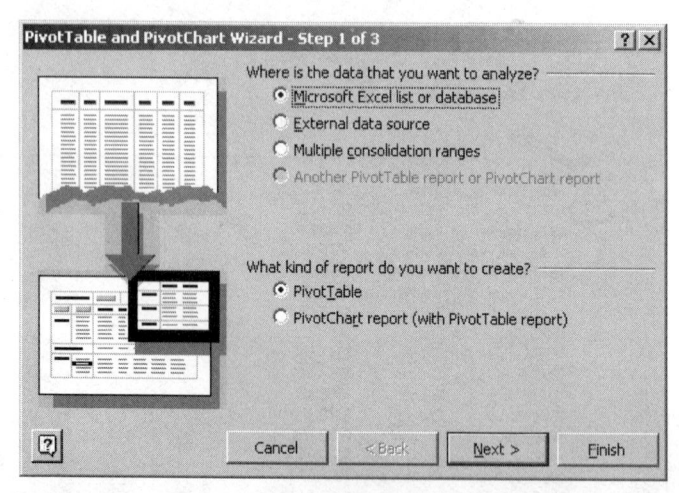

Figure P-6   The first step of the PivotTable And PivotChart Wizard.

2. If your data is in a single range on a single worksheet in the current workbook, click the Microsoft Excel List Or Database option button. Then click the PivotTable option button, and click Next. When the PivotTable And PivotChart Wizard asks you to select the data you want to include in the PivotTable, do so, and then click Next.

3. If your data resides in an external database, click the External Data Source option and Next. Then, when Excel prompts you to identify the external data source, click the Get Data button and use the Choose Data Source dialog box to identify the data.

TIP   *If you want to Pivot data in an external database, ask the database administrator for help. He or she should be able to assist you with identifying and retrieving the data.*

4. If your data resides in multiple ranges or on multiple sheets, click the multiple Consolidation Ranges option and click Next. When Excel asks, indicate how many pages of pivot table information you want.

5. Specify where you want Excel to put the PivotTable you're creating and click Finish. Excel displays the new, empty PivotTable in the location you specified (see Figure P-7). Excel also displays the PivotTable toolbar, which you use to lay out and edit the PivotTable.

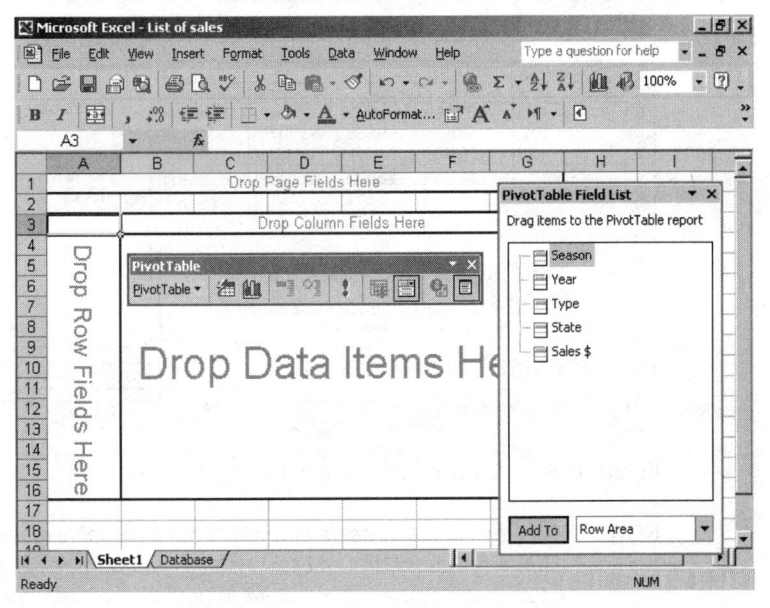

Figure P-7   The new, empty PivotTable and the PivotTable toolbar.

Specifying PivotTable Layout

To begin laying out your PivotTable, use the buttons on the PivotTable toolbar to drag fields to set up row and column headings. In the example shown in Figure P-7, you could drag the Year button to the box labeled Drop Row Fields Here and the State button to the box labeled Drop Column Fields Here. You could then drag the Sales heading to the Drop Data Items Here box. After you drag the Sales button to the Data area, Excel adds the data to the PivotTable (see Figure P-8).

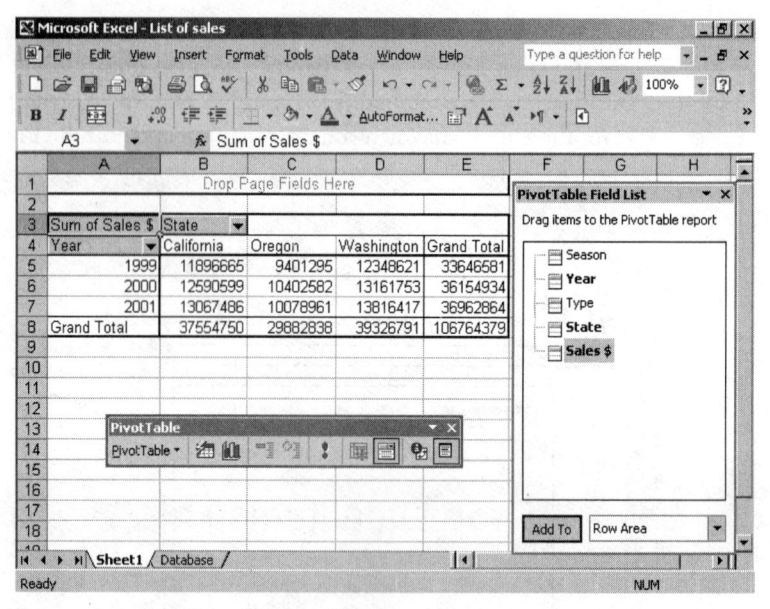

Figure P-8 A PivotTable with data.

NOTE *The box in the upper left corner of the Pivot Table reads Sum Of Sales $. This is because Excel assumes you want to subtotal and total sales figures. If you were to drag a label field instead of a value field into the Data area, Excel would by default count the occurrences of that label.*

You can change the operation performed on the data included in a PivotTable by selecting a cell in the part you want to change and clicking the PivotTable toolbar's Field Settings button. Excel displays the PivotTable Field dialog box (see Figure P-9). This dialog box's options differ slightly depending on the type of data presented in the part of the PivotTable you selected.

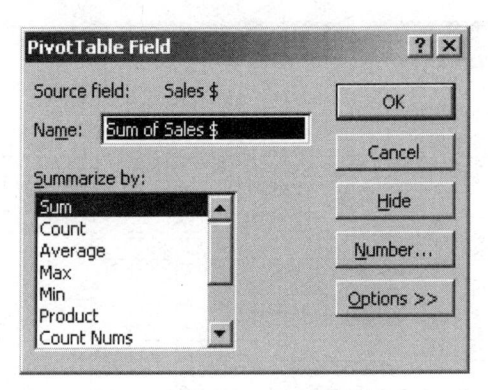

Figure P-9   The PivotTable Field dialog box.

TIP   *To rename a field, enter a new name in the Name text box.*

To change the operation performed on items in the field, select an item from the Summarize By drop-down list box and click OK. For comparative operations, click the Options button. You can then list item data as a percentage of another item, or as a difference from another item, for example.

You can drag multiple fields to a heading. To add another field to a PivotTable, just drag the field's button from the PivotTable toolbar. For example, you could drag the Season field to the right of the Year column to sort by year and then by season (see Figure P-10). To remove a field from a table, just drag the field outside the table area.

P Excel 2002 From A to Z

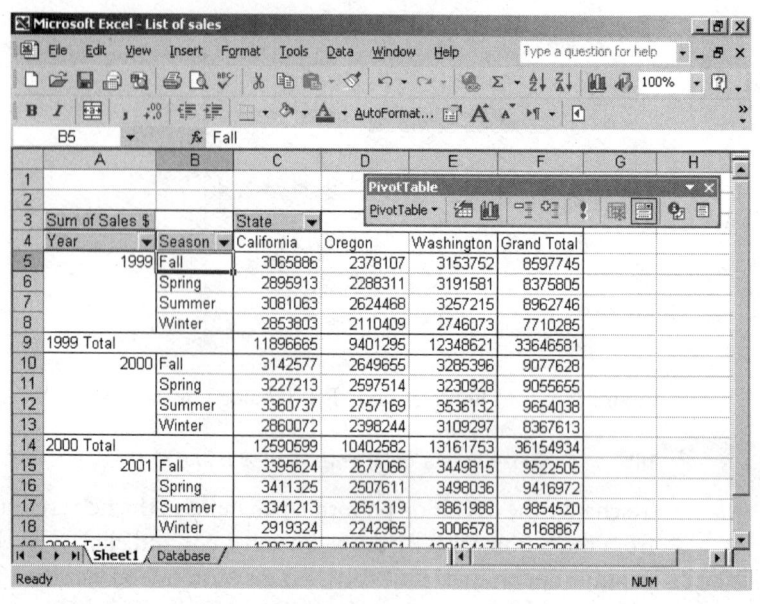

Figure P-10 A PivotTable with multiple row fields.

NOTE   *If you don't see the field buttons on the PivotTable toolbar, click the Display Fields button.*

NOTE   *If you attempt to change the data summarized in a PivotTable (for example, the value in cell D7), Excel prevents you from doing so. This safeguard, of course, is because this cell sums the data for the various types of beer in the list, and you cannot change the sum without changing the values that make up the sum. If you want to change the values in the PivotTable, you must make the changes to the list upon which the PivotTable is based. Then return to the PivotTable and click the Refresh Data button on the PivotTable toolbar to update the PivotTable.*

Editing PivotTables

To pivot a PivotTable, just drag a heading to a different axis. For example, you can drag the Season field to the column heading to create a long, narrow table.

You can also reorganize a PivotTable by changing the hierarchy of fields in a heading. For example, if you look back at the PivotTable in Figure P-10, sales are grouped first by year and then by season within each year. However, if you drag the Season field to the left of the Year field, you can group first by season, and then within each season, by year.

Filtering Items in a Field

You can tell Excel which items you want to include in a PivotTable for each field. For example, if you don't want to worry about sales in California for the moment, you can exclude California from the table. To do so, click the down arrow on the right side of the State heading and clear the California check box. Then click OK.

> TIP   *If your database is so large that your PivotTable is too long or wide to easily read, you can separate data on different pages. Click the PivotTable button on the PivotTable toolbar and choose Show Pages from the pop-up menu to create new sheets in the workbook for each page field. Just select the page field from the list in the Show Pages dialog box, and click OK.*

Creating PivotCharts

To create a PivotChart from an existing PivotTable, select a cell in the PivotTable and click the Chart Wizard button on the PivotTable toolbar.

You manipulate PivotCharts in much the same way as you manipulate PivotTables—by dragging field buttons to different axes (see Figure P-11).

P   Excel 2002 From A to Z

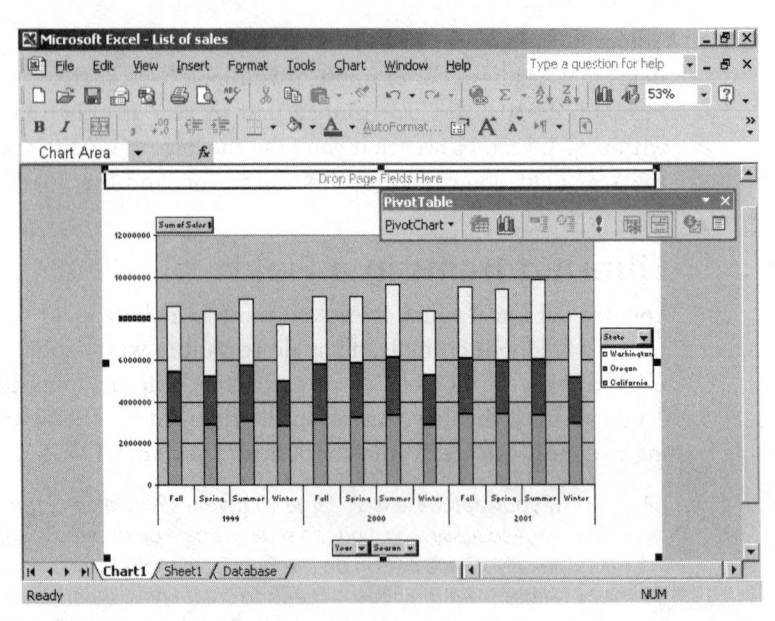

Figure P-11   A Pivot Chart.

You can also filter a PivotChart's data to include only certain items in a field. To do this, click the down arrow on the right side of the field button and select or clear the check boxes to include or omit items from the PivotChart. Click OK to redraw the chart.

After you've created the PivotChart, you can click the Chart Wizard button on the PivotTable toolbar again to start the Chart Wizard and customize the PivotChart. Using the Chart Wizard, you can specify such items as chart type, axis titles, and legend placement.

NOTE   *If you haven't created a PivotTable and are instead more interested in creating a PivotChart, you can create the PivotChart using the PivotTable and PivotChart Wizard without specifying the layout of a PivotTable.*

Point

You specify font size in points because points are the standard unit of measurement in typography. Seventy-two points equal one inch (see Figure P-12). Twelve points equals one pica.

A

Figure P-12   A letter in 72-point type.

Portrait Orientation see Page Orientation

Precedence see Formula Auditing

Previewing Workbooks see Workbooks

Printer Setup

Normally, you set up and configure your printer using the Printers tool, available on the Windows Control Panel. You can also, however, configure your printer from within Excel. To do so, choose the File→Print command and click the Properties command button. When Excel opens the printer's Properties dialog box, use its tabs to make changes to things such as the type of paper the printer uses, the quality at which the printer prints, and the page orientation (see Figure P-13).

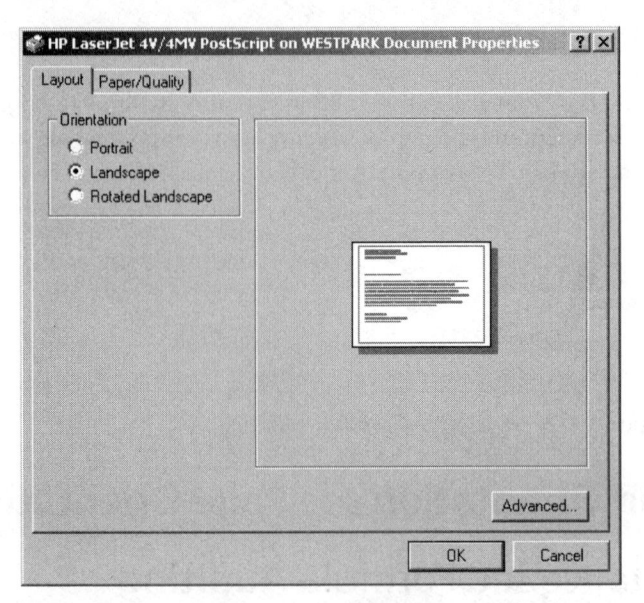

Figure P-13 An example printer properties dialog box.

NOTE   *Different printer's properties dialog boxes look different.*

TIP   *For information on working with your printer's properties dialog box, refer to the printer's documentation.*

Printing Workbooks see Workbooks

Print Queue

Windows shows a print queue, or line, of the documents waiting to print on a printer if you click the Start button, point to the Settings command, click the Printers command, and then double-click the printer (see Figure P-14).

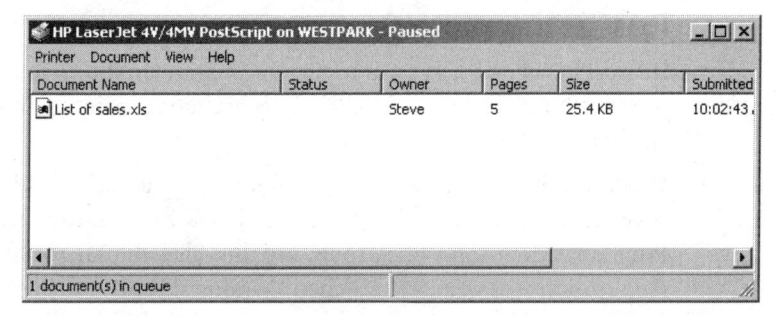

Figure P-14 A printer window.

Depending on your system privileges, you may be able to delete documents from the printer queue or to move documents backwards or forwards in the queue. To delete a workbook, right-click the workbook and choose Cancel from the shortcut menu. To move a workbook forwards or backwards in the queue, right-click the workbook, choose Properties from the shortcut menu and adjust the priority.

SEE ALSO *Documents, Printer Setup*

Privacy Options

You can limit the amount of secondary information stored with a workbook by turning on Excel's privacy options and available to people looking at the unopened workbook file. To do this, choose the Tools→Options command, click the Security tab, and then check the Remove Personal Information From This File On Save box. By checking this box, you tell Excel not to provide summary information about the workbook when someone looks at the file's properties.

SEE ALSO *Password Protecting a Workbook*

Program Errors

Excel program errors will occur. When this happens, either Excel will stop responding, or hang, or Excel will abort and stop. And when any of these things happens, you will typically lose some of your recent work.

Restarting Excel

If Excel has aborted, you can restart the program in the same way that you start Excel. For example, click the Start button, point to Programs, and then click on Microsoft Excel.

When the Excel program stops responding, you may be able to recover the application. To do this, click the Start button, point to Programs, Microsoft Office Tools, and then click the Microsoft Office Application Recovery item. When Windows displays the list of Office programs, select the Excel program and click either the Recover Application or Restart Application button.

> **NOTE** *If you just want to close the unresponsive program, and lose recent changes to the files, click the Start button, point to Programs, Microsoft Office Tools, and click the Microsoft Office Application Recovery item, and then click End Application.*

Recovering Documents

When Excel restarts or recovers after failing or stalling, you need to review the documents listed in the Document Recovery pane. These are the documents that were open when the Excel program error occurred. You'll want to review the recovered documents to find which are worth salvaging, and then save those.

> **NOTE** *In the Document Recovery pane, a file labeled as "recovered" includes more recent changes than the file labeled as "original."*

To open a recovered workbook, point to the workbook in the Document Recovery pane, click the arrow button next to the workbook, and click Open.

To save a workbook, point to the workbook, click the arrow button next to the workbook, and click Save As.

SEE ALSO *Documents*

Program Window

The program window is the rectangle in which the Excel program displays its information. The Microsoft Excel title bar and menu bar appear at the top of the program window. The toolbar or toolbars, located just below the menu bar, provide a series of buttons that allow for faster selection of frequently used menu commands.

Protection

You can format ranges as protected to so that you or somebody else doesn't inadvertently change cell contents.

To format a range as protected, take the following steps:

1. Select the range you want to protect.
2. Choose the Format→Cells command, click the Protection tab, and check the Locked box (see Figure P-15).

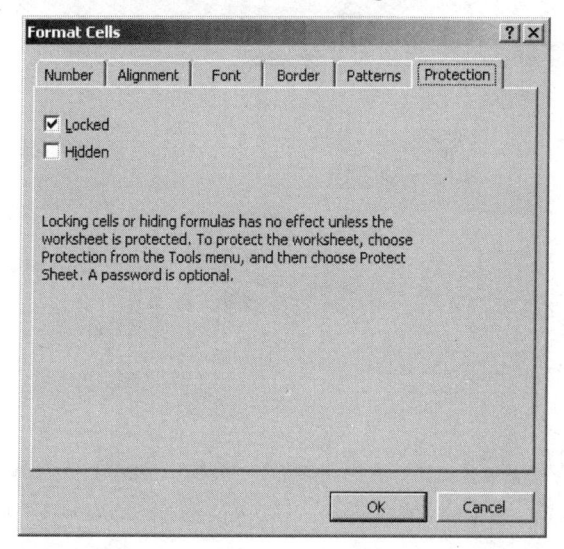

Figure P-15   The Protection tab of the Format Cells dialog box.

3. Choose the Tools→Protection command.

SEE ALSO *Formatting Cells*

Recycle Bin

When you delete an Excel workbook stored on one of your computer's fixed local disk drives, Windows doesn't immediately erase the workbook from the disk. Instead, Windows moves the workbook to the Recycle Bin folder. Eventually, Windows removes the "deleted" workbook from the Recycle Bin (to make room for other, newly "deleted" files) but until that time you can recover the Excel workbook by opening the Recycle Bin folder, selecting the workbook, and choosing the File→Restore command.

R   Excel 2002 From A to Z

SEE ALSO *Workbooks*

Ranges

A range is a rectangle of worksheet cells (see Figure R-1). The smallest range is a single cell. The largest range is an entire worksheet.

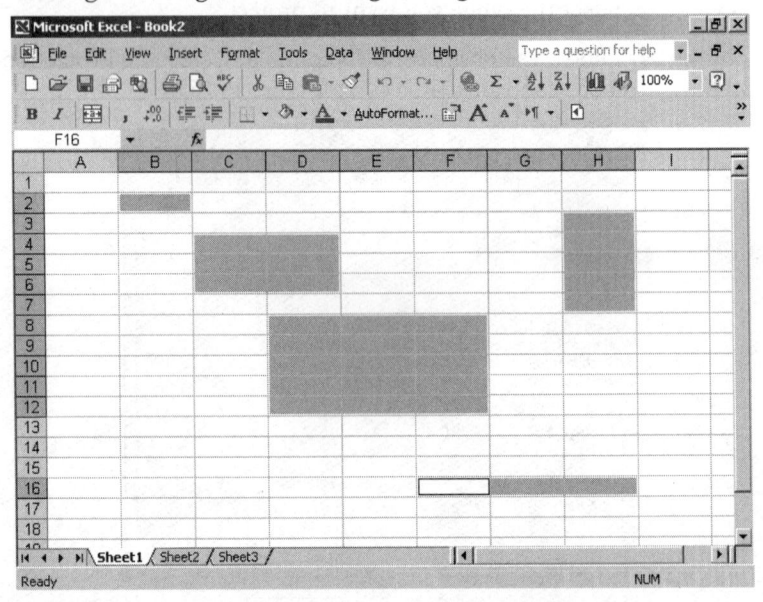

Figure R-1   A worksheet showing several range selections.

To select a range, drag the mouse from one corner of the range to the opposite corner.

You can also specify or reference a range selection by entering the cell addresses of opposite corners separated by the colon. For example, you can reference the range that uses the corner cells A1 and D3 using as A1:D3.

Recalculation

Excel automatically updates the formulas and recalculates their results. For example, if you change the value in cell C1 from 500 to 600, Excel recalculates any formulas that use the value stored in cell C1.

In simple worksheets with a few formulas, recalculation takes place so quickly you won't even be aware it's occurring. In larger worksheets

136

with hundreds or thousands of formulas, recalculation may seem slower. The mouse pointer changes to the hourglass symbol when Excel is busy recalculating.

If you don't want Excel to automatically recalculate formulas as you're working, choose the Tools→Options command and click the Calculation tab. Then click the Manual option button under Calculation, and click OK. The word Calculate appears on the status bar when your worksheet formulas need to be recalculated. You can force recalculation by pressing the F9 key.

SEE ALSO *Formulas*

Redo see Undoing Mistakes

#REF Message see Error Messages

Relative Cell Addresses see Copying Formulas

Renaming Sheets see Sheets

Replacing Cell Contents

When you choose the Edit→Replace command, Excel displays the Replace tab of the Find And Replace dialog box (see Figure R-2).

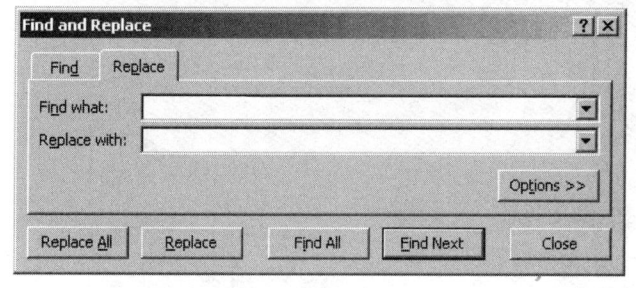

Figure R-2 The Replace tab of the Find And Replace dialog box.

Enter the label, value or formula you want to find in the Find What text box and the label, value, or formula with which you want to replace it in the Replace With text box.

Click Find Next and Replace to search for and replace entries one by one. Or click Replace All to have Excel automatically find and replace all occurrences of the entry without requesting verification from you. Click Close when you're finished.

> **NOTE** *If you click the Options button Excel adds several boxes and buttons to the Find And Replace dialog box, which you can use to control how Excel searches the workbook. For information on these options, refer to the Finding Cell Contents entry.*

Resizing Objects see Sizing Objects

Resizing Text see Formatting Cells

Resizing Windows see Sizing Windows

Revisions

Excel tracks revisions to shared workbooks. To turn on change tracking and workbook sharing, choose the Tools→Track Changes command. When Excel displays the Highlight Changes dialog box, check the Track Changes While Editing Box (see Figure R-3)

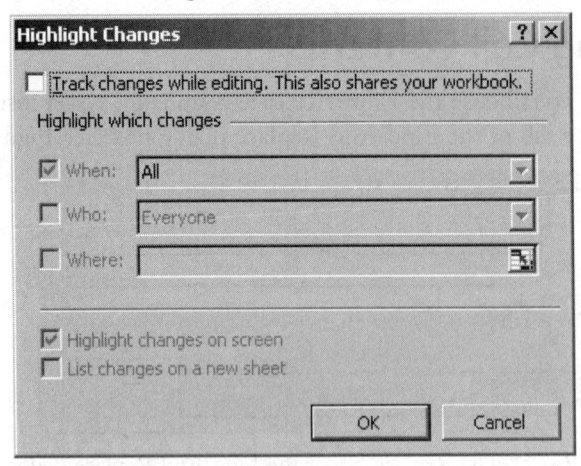

Figure R-3 The Highlight Changes dialog box.

Once change tracking is turned on, edits to a workbook show in a different color.

Excel 2002 From A to Z

To review changes, choose the Tools→Track Changes→Accept Or Reject Changes command. Excel displays the Accept or Reject Changes dialog box, which you use to see each change and then decide whether to accept or reject the change. (see Figure R-4).

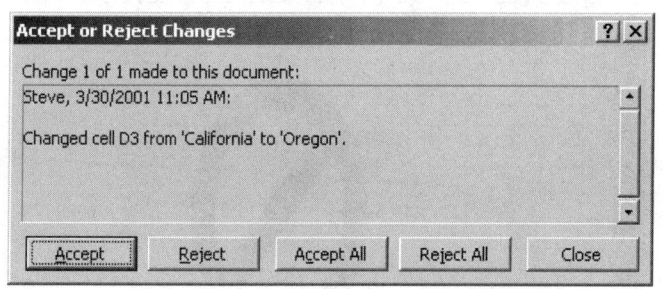

Figure R-4   The Accept Or Reject Changes dialog box.

SEE ALSO *Sharing Excel Workbooks*

Rotating Objects

You can rotate, or spin, many of the objects you place in an Excel workbook. To do so, click the object to select. Then, drag the green selection handle (see Figure R-5).

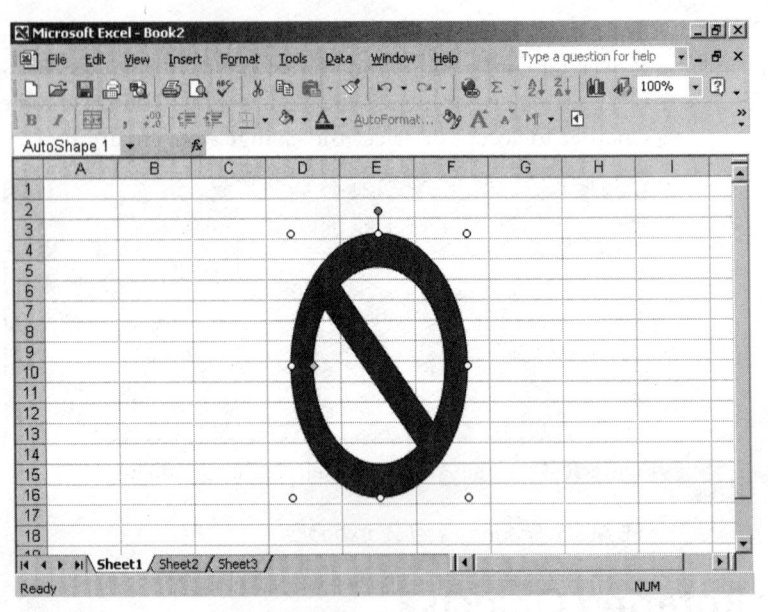

Figure R-5   A selected autoshape object.

SEE ALSO *Drawing*

Rows

The left edge of the workbook window identifies each row in your worksheet using numbers. An Excel worksheet can have up to 65,536 rows.

Normally, Excel automatically increases row height when you increase point size, but you can perform the same trick on rows by double-clicking the lower border of a row heading. This expands the row to the smallest height possible that still fits all entries within that row.

To specify exact row height, select any cell in that row and choose the Format→Row→Height command. Enter the height in points in the Row Height text box, and click OK.

To hide a row, select any cell in the row and choose the Format→Row→Hide command. To redisplay a hidden row, select a range that includes cells in the rows above and below the hidden row. Then choose the Format→Row→Unhide command.

Saving Workbooks see Workbooks

Scenarios

Scenarios let you perform what-if analysis by changing several worksheet input values at a time and exploring the effect on large numbers of formulas.

Creating a Scenario

To use Scenario Manager, follow these steps:

1. Choose the Tools→Scenarios command.
2. When Excel displays the Scenario Manager dialog box, click the Add button so that Excel displays the Add Scenario dialog box (see Figure S-1).

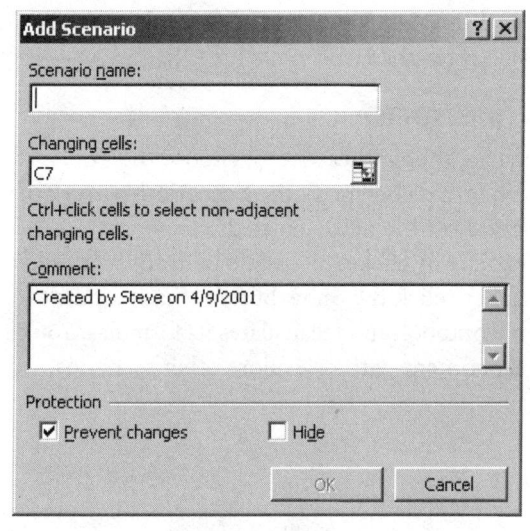

Figure S-1   The Add Scenario dialog box.

3. Give the scenario a name by typing a description in the Scenario Name text box.
4. Enter the worksheet range that holds the cells you want to change in the Changing Cells text box of the Add Scenario dialog box by using the mouse to select the worksheet range. If you want to enter several worksheet ranges, hold down the Ctrl key as you select ranges. When you finish, click OK. Excel displays the Scenario Values dialog box (see Figure S-2).

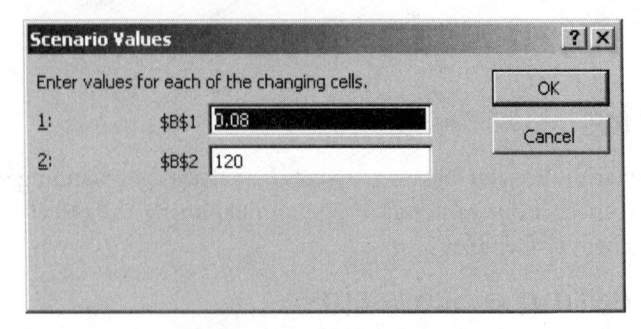

Figure S-2 The Scenario Values dialog box.

5. Enter the input value you want to use for each scenario value. If you've selected more input cells than will fit within the Scenario Values dialog box, you'll need to scroll through the list. Click OK when you finish. Excel redisplays the Add Scenario dialog box.

Repeat steps 2 through 5 to create additional scenarios. After you complete step 5 for the last time, click OK.

Using a Scenario

To use a scenario, follow these steps, choose the Tools→Scenarios command. When Excel displays the Scenario Manager dialog box, which will now show the newly created scenario, select the scenario you want to explore by clicking its name in the Scenarios list box (see Figure S-3). Then, click the Show button. Excel inputs the scenario values in your workbook and recalculates its formulas. You can repeat this step to experiment with or explore other scenarios.

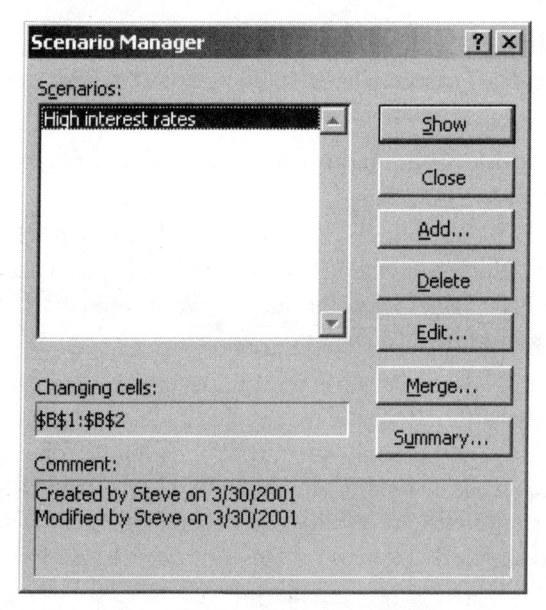

Figure S-3 The Scenario Manager dialog box.

Editing a Scenario

To remove an existing scenario, choose the Tools→Scenarios command so that Excel displays the Scenario Manager dialog box. Then select the scenario you want to delete, and click Delete.

To edit an existing scenario, choose the Tools→Scenarios command. Select the scenario you want to edit and click the Edit button so that Excel displays the Edit Scenario dialog box. Edit the scenario name by editing the contents of the Scenario Name text box. Change the scenario inputs by editing or replacing the worksheet range or worksheet ranges shown in the Changing Cells text box of the Edit Scenario dialog box. Click OK. When Excel displays the Scenario Values dialog box, use it to change the scenario's input values.

Summarizing Scenarios

To create summary of scenarios either on a separate worksheet or using a PivotTable, follow these steps:

1. Choose the Tools→Scenarios command. Excel displays the Scenario Manager dialog box.
2. Click the Summary button. Excel displays the Scenario Summary dialog box, which asks whether you want to display a scenario summary or a PivotTable. Select the button that corresponds to the type of scenario summary you want.
3. Specify which Result cells you want to see in the summary—these are the cells with the formulas that change as you explore different scenarios—by selecting them with the mouse. You can select nonadjacent cells by holding down the Ctrl key as you click. Click OK when you finish. Excel adds a scenario summary to your workbook that shows the scenario values and the selected Result cells (see Figure S-4).

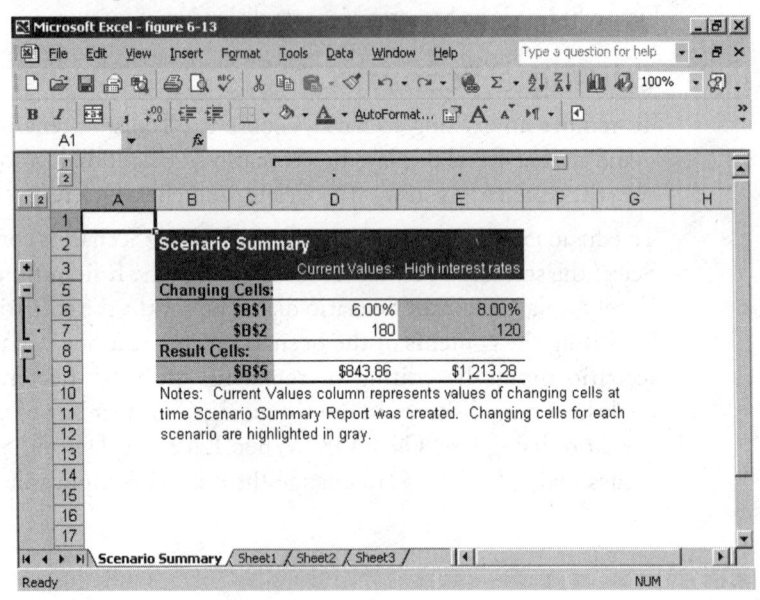

Figure S-4 A Scenario Summary worksheet.

Merging Scenarios from Other Workbooks

If two workbooks use the same set of input cells, you can copy, or merge, a scenario from one open workbook to another open workbook. To merge scenarios, open and activate the workbook to which you'll add a scenario. Choose the Tools→Scenarios command and click the Merge button. Use the Book list box to select the workbook from which you want to retrieve a scenario, and use the Sheet list box to select the scenario you want to retrieve. Then click OK. Excel merges the scenarios from the source workbook into the active workbook. You can now use these scenarios in the same way as those you create from scratch.

Scientific Notation

If a value is too large to fit into a single cell, Excel either increases the cell width or displays the cell contents using scientific notation. The number 1234567890, for example, may appear as 1.23456E+9. Likewise, the number .0000000001 may appear as something like 1E-10.

Excel doesn't discard the extra digits if they don't fit in the cell. If you select the cell, you can see all of the digits in the formula bar. One exception to this rule concerns extremely large or extremely small values. Excel uses only the first 15 digits of a value. If you enter a value that uses more than 15 digits, Excel rewrites the value using only 15 digits. If the value uses more than 20 digits, Excel rewrites the value using scientific notation. If the value uses more than 15 digits but less than 20 digits, Excel replaces the sixteenth digit through the twentieth digit (counting from left to right) with zeros and then drops the zeros if they aren't significant. For example, the value 12345678901234567890 is rewritten to 12345678901234500000. And the value .12345678901234567890 is rewritten to .123456789012345.

SEE ALSO *Values*

Scrolling

You have several methods for scrolling through the Excel workbook shown in the document window:

- You can use the workbook window's scroll bar. This scroll bar works like other scroll bars in Windows. You can click the arrows at either end of the scroll bar to scroll in the direction of the arrow. You can drag the scroll bar marker in the direction you want to scroll. You can also click above or below the scroll bar marker to move the marker in the direction you click.

- You can use the up and down arrow keys to move one line in the direction of arrow and the Page Up and Page Down keys to move one page up or down.

- You can use the Edit→Go To command to jump to a range or cell in a workbook.

SEE ALSO *Go To*

Selecting Objects

Typically, you can select any object by clicking the object with the mouse. Note, though, that if an object is created by another program (an Excel chart, say) or by an applet (a piece of WordArt, for example), you may need to double-click the object in order to simultaneously open and select the object.

Selecting Ranges

You can select ranges with the mouse or the keyboard. To use the mouse, drag the mouse between the range's opposite corners. To use the keyboard, first move the cell selector to one of the corners, then hold down the Shift key and press the arrow keys or the Page Up and Page Down key to highlight the range you want.

NOTE   *To select multiple ranges using the mouse, hold down the Ctrl key as you drag to make your selections.*

SEE ALSO *Ranges*

Series see Charts

Shading see Formatting Cells

Shadows

To add shadows to the selected range, choose the Format→Font command, click the Font tab, and check the Shadow box.

SEE ALSO *Fonts*

Sharing Excel Workbooks

You can share an Excel workbook so that more than one person can open the workbook and make changes. To share, choose the Tools→Share Workbook command. When Excel displays the Share Workbook dialog box, click the Editing tab and check the Allow Changes By More Than One User box (see Figure S-5).

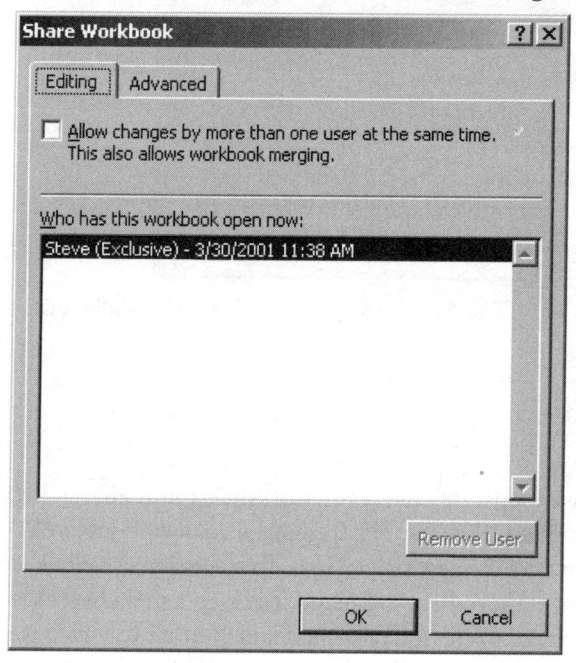

Figure S-5   The Editing tab of the Share Workbook dialog box.

The Advanced tab of the Share Workbook dialog box provides buttons and boxes you use to describe how Excel monitors and reconciles changes to the workbook (see Figure S-6). The Track Changes buttons, for example, let you tell Excel for how long it should keep a record of changes. The Update Changes buttons let you specify when Excel should save the workbook changes. The Conflicting Changes Between Users buttons let you specify which changes take precedence if changes conflict.

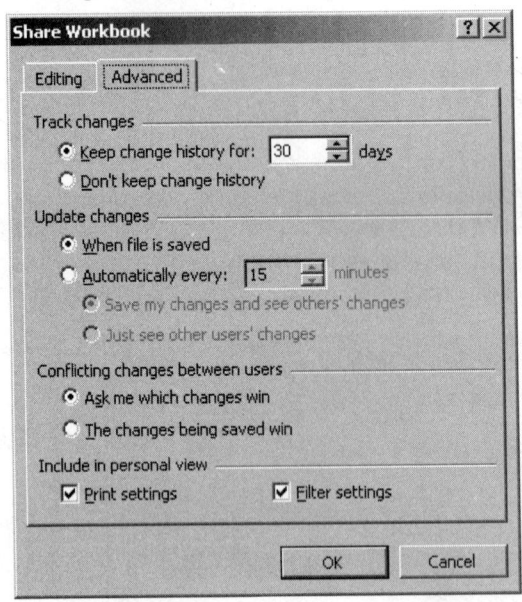

Figure S-6   The Advanced tab of the Share Workbook dialog box.

SEE ALSO *Revisions*

Sheets

Excel uses separate sheets for worksheets and charts. To move to another sheet, click its tab. To rename a sheet, double-click the tab and then type the new sheet name. To insert a new worksheet, choose the Insert→Worksheet command. To insert a new chart sheet, use the ChartWizard to create a new chart and indicate you want to place the chart on its own sheet. To delete a sheet, right-click its tab and choose Delete from the shortcut menu.

TIP   *When you right-click a sheet tab, Excel displays a shortcut menu of several useful commands for working with sheets, including commands for renaming a sheet, moving or copying the sheet, and coloring the sheet's tab.*

Shortcut Menus

Recent Microsoft programs, including Microsoft Excel, make use of shortcut menus. A shortcut menu lists all of the common commands for working on a particular object or item. To display a shortcut menu, right-click the object or item.

Sizing Objects

Usually, you can size an object, such as a picture, a piece of WordArt, or a drawing object, by clicking the object to select it and then dragging the selection handles.

SEE ALSO *Clip Art, Pictures, WordArt*

Sizing Text see Formatting Cells

Sizing Windows

You can size and resize the Excel program window by clicking the Minimize, Maximize, and Restore buttons. These buttons appear in the upper left corner of the Excel program window.

SEE ALSO *Active Document Window, Application Window, Control Menu*

Smart Tags

Excel can recognize some of the information in your workbook—typically data such as people's names and phone numbers. When Excel does recognize something, it marks the information with a smart tag, which appears as purple underline. If you point to the smart tag, Excel displays the Smart Tab Actions button which you can click to display a menu of commands you can choose to use the data in same way. A person's name that Excel smart tags, for example, could be added to names and address line maintained in Microsoft Outlook. Smart tags are useful, then, because they let you do things in Excel that normally you would have to open another program to do.

To turn on the smart tags feature, choose the Tools→AutoCorrect Options command, click the Smart Tags tab, and check the Label Text With Smart Tags box (see Figure S-7).

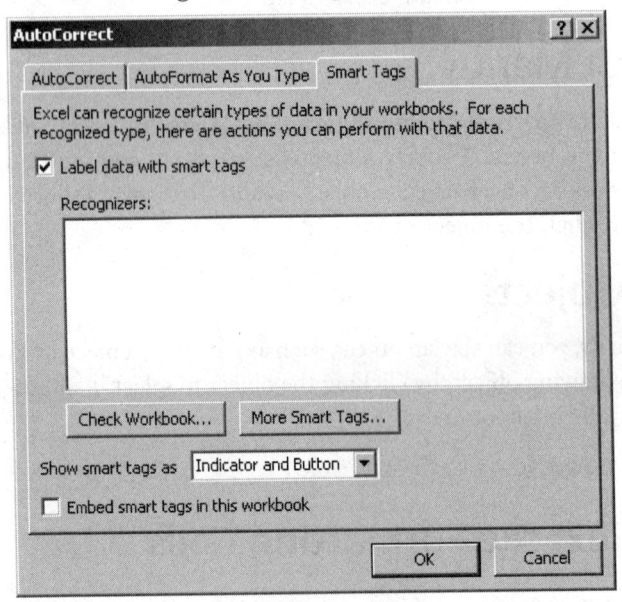

Figure S-7 The Smart Tags tab of the AutoCorrect dialog box.

Solver

Excel's Solver tool lets you solve optimization-modeling problems, also commonly known as linear programming programs. With an optimization-modeling problem, you want to optimize an objective function but at the same time recognize that there are constraints, or limits. Using Solver for optimization modeling requires a lengthy discussion and therefore isn't covered here. Refer to a large Excel reference if you want more information, such as the *MBA's Guide to Microsoft Excel 2002* (Redmond Technology Press 2001).

Sorting Lists see Lists

Speech Recognition

Excel 2002 includes speech recognition. This new tool requires some set up time and bit of getting used to, but for some people, the work pays off. Speech recognition, for some people, can be a huge timesaver.

Excel 2002 From A to Z   **S**

TIP   *Speech Recognition requires a good quality headset microphone, at least a 400MHz computer and at least 128MB of memory.*

Setting Up Speech Recognition

To set up Speech Recognition, you need to configure your microphone and then train Speech Recognition to recognize your particular voice.

To configure the microphone, click the Start button, choose the Settings→Control Panel command, and double-click the Speech tool. Windows displays the Speech Properties dialog box (see Figure S-8).

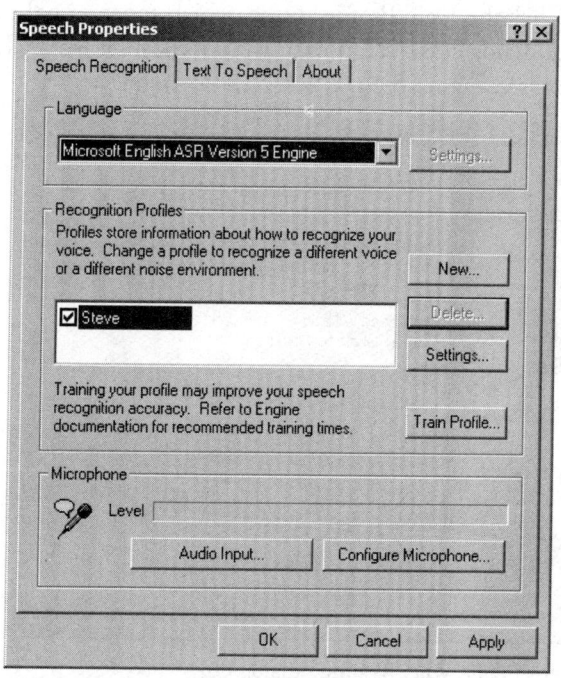

Figure S-8   The Speech Properties dialog box.

Put the headset on and position the microphone so that it's about an inch from your mouth. Click Configure Microphone and then Next. Windows will instruct you to read some text to adjust the microphone volume and then, when that's done, Windows instructs you to read a simple sentence, "This papaya tastes perfect." Windows then plays a recording of you saying "This papaya tastes perfect." If the recording sounds okay, you're done and click Finish. If the recording sounds funny, move the microphone away from or close to your mouth.

S

Excel 2002 From A to Z

NOTE   *If you click the Microphone button on the Language bar and haven't yet configured the Microphone, you'll be prompted to walk through the steps for both configuring the microphone and training speech recognition to understand your voice. In this case, you don't need to use the Control Panel's Speech tool to get to the Speech Properties dialog box. The Language bar gets you there.*

After you configure the microphone, you need to train the Speech Recognition tool to recognize your voice. To do this, click Start, point to Settings and choose Control Panel. Then, double-click the Speech tool and Click the Train Profile button, which appears on the Speech Properties dialog box. Windows displays the first Voice Training dialog box (see Figure S-9). Click Next to begin.

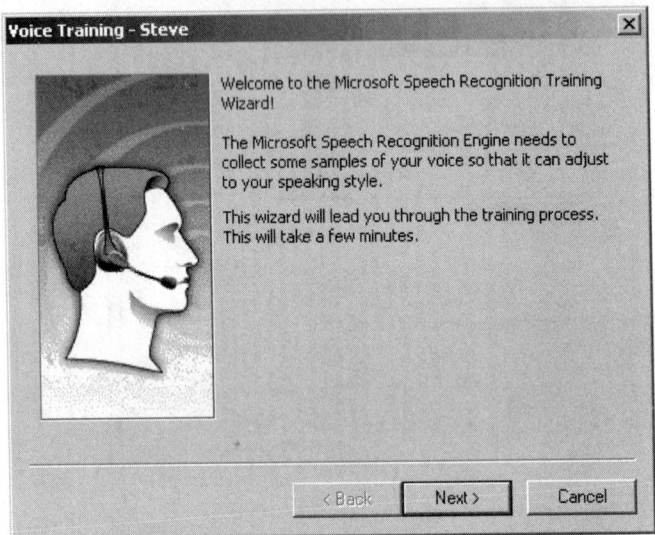

Figure S-9   The Voice Training dialog box.

To train the speech recognition tool to recognize your speech, you first answer questions about your age and sex. Then, you read a short description of speech recognition technology. As you read the short description, Speech Recognition highlights words as you say them and it recognizes them. Make sure that Speech Recognition does this. If speech recognition doesn't recognize a word, try speaking more slowly and clearly. If you can't get Speech Recognition to understand your pronunciation of a word, click the Skip Word button.

> NOTE   The reading you do to train Speech Recognition is very short. You can finish it in about five minutes. However, if you need to take a break, click the Pause button.

Using Speech Recognition

Once you configure your microphone and train speech recognition to understand your voice, you can begin to enter information or choose commands. These appear on the Language Bar (see Figure S-10). Click the Microphone button and then the Dictation button to enter information. Click the Microphone button and then the Voice Command button to choose commands by speaking. Then, begin speaking in a normal voice. As you talk, speech recognition interprets your words and enters them into the workbook at the insertion point or chooses the commands.

To begin entering information into a cell, say the word "Enter."

When you say a number, Speech Recognition spells out numbers less than twenty. For example, say "five" and Speech Recognition interprets this as the word *five*, but say "twenty-five" and Speech Recognition interprets this as the number *25*. Speech Recognition will recognize fractions. For example, if you say "one-half," Speech Recognition interprets this as ½.

To tell Speech Recognition to interpret what you're saying as values, say "force num," pause, and then say your values. In this case, if you say "five," Speech Recognition interprets this as the value "5."

If Speech Recognition doesn't understand, click the Correction button and see if another interpretation of what you said is listed. If it is, select the alternative interpretation by clicking.

Or, you can select the incorrect text and then began speaking again. If speech recognition understands, it replaces the incorrect selected text with the new corrected text.

When you finish dictating, click the Microphone button again.

To use speech recognition for voice commands, click the Microphone button and then click the Voice Command button. Then, choose commands and select dialog box options by speaking. For example, to print your workbook, say, "File Print OK." To change the font used for the selected worksheet range to Helvetica, say, "Format Font Helvetica."

Punctuating Your Speech

Most of the words you say will be recognized as input as words. In the case of characters used for punctuation, however, Excel assumes you mean punctuation. The table below shows punctuation symbols and lists the words you can use to enter them:

SYMBOL	WORD
.	Period or Dot
,	Comma
:	Colon
;	Semi-colon
?	Question mark
!	Exclamation point
&	Ampersand
*	Asterisk
@	At sign
\	Backslash
/	Slash
|	Vertical bar
-	Hyphen or Dash
—	Double dash
=	Equals
+	Plus or Plus sign
#	Pound sign
%	Percent sign
$	Dollar sign
_	Underscore
~	Tilde
...	Ellipsis
>	Greater than

<	Less than
^	Caret
[	Bracket or Left bracket or Open bracket
]	End bracket or Right bracket or Close bracket
{	Open brace or Curly brace or Left brace
}	Close brace or End curly brace or Right brace
(	Open parenthesis or Left paren
)	Close parenthesis or Right paren
"	Quote or Open quote or Close Quote
'	Single quote or Open single quote or Close single quote

Customizing Speech Recognition

The Language bar's Speech Tools button displays a menu of commands you can use to customize the way that Speech Recognition works.

- To reconfigure your microphone or create a new speech profile, click the Options command. Excel displays the Speech Properties dialog box—the same one you worked with to originally configure the microphone and train.

- To turn off the speech messages that Speech Recognition displays on the Language bar—messages that might say you're speaking to soft, too loud, or too quickly—choose the Show Speech Messages command. The Show Speech Messages command is toggle switch. When speech messages show, a check mark shows in front in the command name.

- To further train Speech Recognition so it will do a better job recognizing your words, choose the Train command. When Excel displays the Voice Training dialog box, select one of the training sessions and then perform the reading. The more you train, the better Speech Recognition works.

- To add or delete words in the speech dictionary, click the Add/Delete Words command. Excel displays the Add/Delete Words dialog box. To delete a word, scroll through the list of words, click the word you want to delete, and then click the Delete button. To add a word, enter the word into the Word box, click the Record Pronunciation button, and then say the word. To record your pronunciation of a word that Speech Recognition commonly misinterprets, select the word in the list, click the Record Pronunciation button, and then say the word.

- To permanently save the recorded speech—normally your recorded speech is only saved until you close the workbook—choose the Save Speech data command. The Save Speech Data command is a toggle switch. To later turn off the saving of your recorded speech data, choose the command again. (Note that you may also need to choose the Tools→Options command, click the Save tab, and then check the Embed Linguistic Data box so save your recorded speech.)

- To select another user's speech profile, click the Current User button and select another speaker profile from the list.

SEE ALSO *Handwriting Recognition*

Spelling

You can also use the Tools→Spelling command to check spelling in your workbooks. When you choose the command, Excel displays the Spelling dialog box (see Figure S-10). Excel identifies misspelled words in the Not In Dictionary box. In the Suggestions box, Excel suggests solutions. To make a suggested fix, double-click it. To ignore the error, click the Ignore button. To add the word to a custom dictionary because it is correctly spelled and you will use it again and again in your documents, click the Add To Dictionary button.

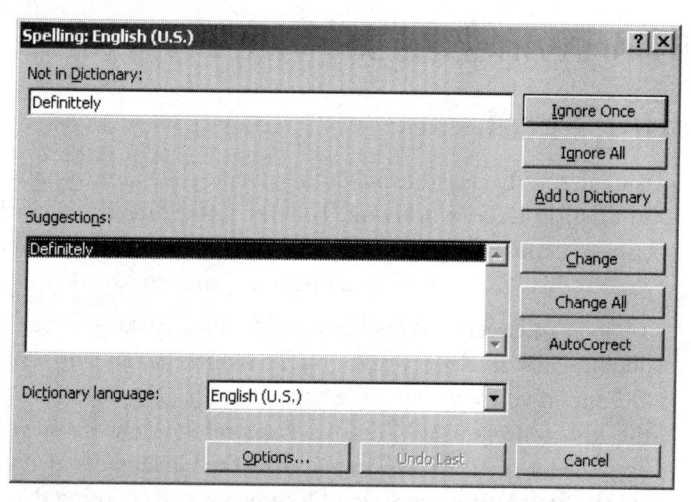

Figure S-10 The Spelling dialog box.

The Options button on the Spelling And Grammar box displays the Spelling dialog box. (You can also get to this tab of options by choosing the Tools→Options command and clicking the Spelling tab.)

- Use the Dictionary Language box to select the dictionary you want to use for checking the spelling.

- Select the dictionary that Excel should add new words to using the Add Words To box.

- Check the Suggest From Main Dictionary Only box to tell Excel to only use the main Excel dictionary for spell checking.

- Check the Ignore Words In UPPERCASE box to tell Excel it should ignore words that use all uppercase letters (presumably because these are acronyms or abbreviations that won't be in the dictionary).

- Check the Ignore Words With Numbers to tell Excel that it should ignore words that combine letters and numbers (presumably because you're using things like product names or serial numbers that won't be in the dictionary).

- Check the Ignore Internet And File Addresses box to tell Excel it should ignore Internet URLs and file pathnames when it checks spelling.

SEE ALSO *Dictionary*

Splitting Windows see Window Panes

Starting Excel

You can start Excel either by starting the program directly or by opening an existing Excel workbook. To start Excel directly, click the Start button, choose Programs, and then choose Microsoft Excel. When you do this, Excel starts and opens a blank workbook.

To open an Excel workbook—which indirectly starts Excel—you can double-click an Excel workbook file (which has an icon with a green "X" and, if you're viewing file extensions, has the extension .XLS) in the My Computer or Windows Explorer window. If you've recently used the file, you can also open it from the Documents menu by clicking the Start button, choosing Documents, and choosing the Excel file you want to open. When you do this, Excel starts and opens the workbook you selected.

> **NOTE** *You can also create shortcuts that point to the Excel program or to Excel workbooks. When you open a shortcut, Windows starts the program or opens the workbook that the shortcut points to. For information on creating and using shortcuts, refer to the Windows help file.*

SEE ALSO *Documents, Program Errors, Stopping Excel*

Status Bar

At the bottom of the program window, Excel displays a status bar. This bar provides information such as whether the worksheet needs to be recalculated and whether Excel is recording a macro.

Stopping Excel

To stop the Excel program, choose the File→Exit command or click the Excel program window's Close box. The Close box is the small square marked with an "X" in the upper left corner of the program window.

SEE ALSO *Starting Excel*

Styles

A style is a collection of formatting settings. By applying the style, you make all of the formatting changes included in the style.

Applying Styles

To apply a style to the selected range, choose the Format→Style command so that Excel displays the Style dialog box (see Figure S-11). Then, select the style from the Style Name box and click OK.

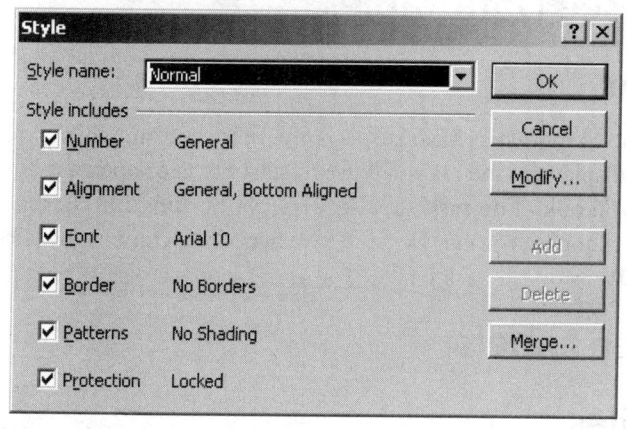

Figure S-11 The Style dialog box.

You can also apply a style by selecting a range that already has the style, clicking the Format Painter tool, and then selecting the range to which you want to apply the style.

Creating a Style

To create a style, choose the Format→Styles command. When Excel displays the Styles dialog box, enter a name for the style into the Style Name box, check the boxes that correspond to the type of formatting you want to include in the style, and then click the Add button.

Modifying a Style

To modify a style, choose the Format→Styles command, select the style from the Style Name box, and click the Modify button. When Excel displays the Format Cells dialog box, use it to make your changes.

Deleting a Style

To delete a style, choose the Format→Styles command, select the style from the Style Name box, and click the Delete button.

SEE ALSO *Formatting Cells*

Subtotaling Lists see Lists

Tables see Data Tables

Taskbar

The Windows taskbar displays the Start button, which you can use to display the menus you'll use to start Excel or open a recently-used workbook. The taskbar also displays buttons for the open Excel workbooks. You can switch between open documents by clicking the buttons on the task bar.

Text see Labels

Text Files

Excel lets you easily import textual data into an Excel workbook. Anything you can get as a text file—such as a financial report generated by the mainframe accounting system—can be imported into Excel and then examined.

To import a text file into Excel, follow these steps:

1. Using the File→Open command, tell Excel that you want to open the text file. When Excel displays the Open dialog box, select the All Files item or the Text File items in the List Files Of Type box so that your text file is listed. Once you find the file, click it and then click the Open button. Excel displays the first Text Import Wizard dialog box (see Figure T-1).

Excel 2002 From A to Z   T

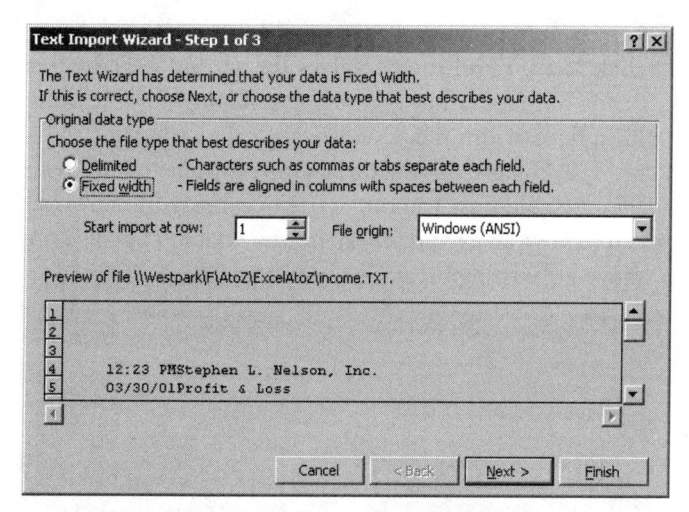

Figure T-1 The first Text Import Wizard dialog box.

2. Use the Original Data Type option buttons—Fixed Width or Delimited—to indicate whether the file uses a fixed-width format, which is the same thing as a straight text file, or uses delimiting characters. Excel can usually guess correctly about which format your text file uses, so if you're not sure which option to select, accept Excel's default suggestion.

3. Use the Start Import At Row box to indicate which row of the text file is the first row you want to have imported. For example, you might not want to import reader header and title information, and might instead want only to begin importing the first row with the data.

4. Use the File Origin box to identify the source of the file. If you're importing data created by another Windows program, select the Windows (ANSI) entry from the File Origin box. If you're importing data from a mainframe, select the MS-DOS (PC-8) entry from the File Origin box.

> **NOTE**   *You can use the Preview box to see how Excel interprets your to-be-imported data.*

T

Excel 2002 From A to Z

5. Once you finish with the first Text Import Wizard dialog box, you click Next. Excel then displays the second Text Import Wizard dialog box (see either Figure T-2 or Figure T-3). If you're importing a fixed-width file, Excel displays the dialog box shown in Figure T-2. You use this dialog box to verify how Excel breaks the text file into columns. You can create new break lines by clicking. You can remove an existing break line by double-clicking. You can also move an existing break line by dragging.

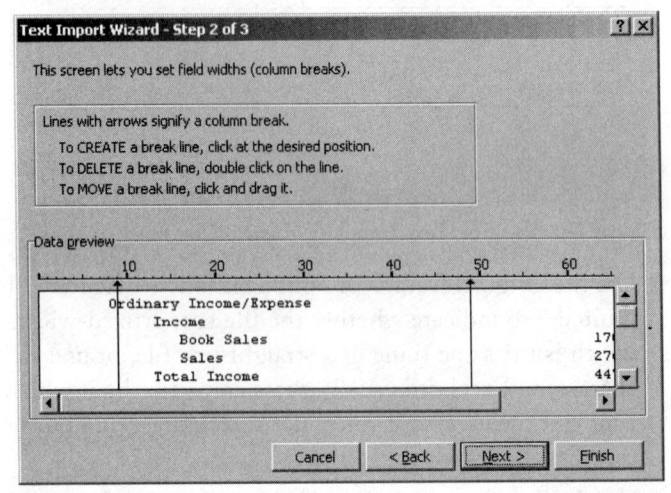

Figure T-2   The second Text Import Wizard dialog box if you're importing a fixed-width file.

If you're importing a delimited character file, Excel displays the dialog box shown in Figure T-3. You use this dialog box principally to verify that Excel has correctly identified the delimiter: The checked Delimiters box should identify the delimiter. You can also indicate if the text file uses a character (such as a quotation mark) to identify text. Note that you can tell whether Excel's delimiter assumptions correctly describe the text file because the preview box shows how your data look given the delimiter specifications.

Excel 2002 From A to Z   T

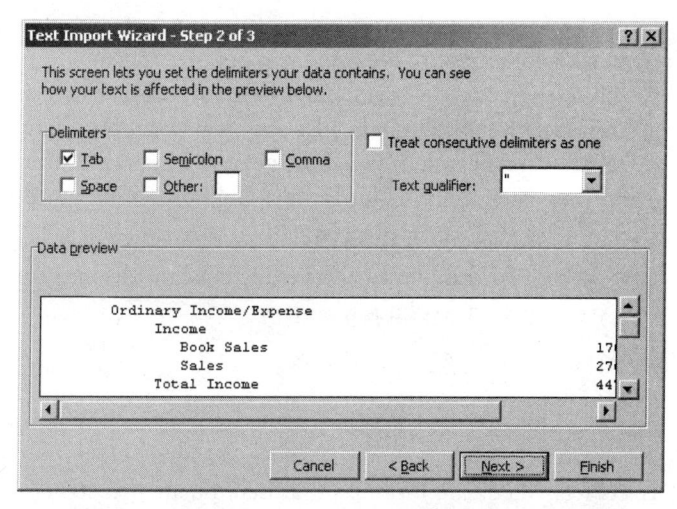

Figure T-3   The second Text Import Wizard dialog box if you're importing a delimited character file.

6. After you've verified the fixed-width or delimited character assumptions of Excel—and fixed any incorrect assumptions—click Next. Excel displays the third Text Import Wizard (see Figure T-4). You use this dialog box to specify the formatting assumptions Excel should make about the to-be-imported text file.

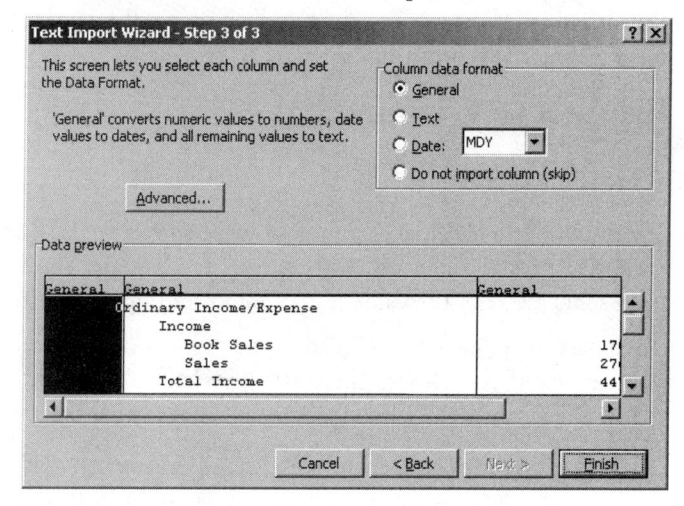

Figure T-4   The third Text Import Wizard dialog box.

163

Excel also guesses about the default formatting that it should use for each column of the text file you import. You should verify that each column uses the best default formatting. To change a column's format, click the column header and then the appropriate Column Data Format button. If you don't want to import a column, click it and then click the Do Not Import Column option button.

7. Click Finish and Excel imports the text file into a new, blank, open workbook. At this point, you're ready to begin cleaning up the data so you can start working with it.

SEE ALSO *Workbooks*

Text Formulas

Excel lets you create formulas that manipulate text strings. Most of these text formulas use functions. For example, the function =PROPER("winston churchill") capitalizes the first letter of each word included in the text argument, returning *Winston Churchill*. And the function =REPT("Bora",2) repeats the first text argument the number of times specified in the second argument, returning *BoraBora*.

Excel also supplies a concatenation operator, &, that allows you to concatenate, or combine, text enclosed in quotation marks. For example, the formula ="Microsoft"&" "&"Excel" combines the word Microsoft, a space, and the word Excel into the text string *Microsoft Excel*.

SEE ALSO *Formulas*

Times and Time Values

Excel uses decimal values to represent times so you can easily perform time-based math. The value .0 represents 12:00am, the value .25 represents 6:00am, the value .5 represents 12:00pm, and so on.

To make time values easier to read, Excel supplies time formats, which you can see if you choose the Format→Cells command, click the Number tab, and select Time from the Category list box.

> **NOTE** *Excel uses integers for date values, so you can combine date integer values and time decimal values to create precise date and time values.*

Toolbars

Excel provides nineteen different toolbars. Each supplies a set of clickable buttons and boxes you can use to easily choose commands and use Excel features. The standard toolbar, for example, includes buttons for printing, spelling, and undoing.

Identifying Toolbar Tools

To identify a toolbar button or box, point to the tool. Excel displays a pop-up box, called a tool tip or screentip, with the tool's name.

Displaying and Removing Toolbars

Typically, Excel displays a toolbar when you're working with items that toolbar supplies tools for. For example, if working with a WordArt object, Excel displays the WordArt toolbar.

You can also control when a toolbar is displayed. Simply choose the View→Toolbars command and then select the toolbar you want. The commands listed on the Toolbars submenu are toggle switches. Excel places a checkmark in front of those toolbars that are displayed. To remove a toolbar, choose the View→Toolbars command and select the displayed toolbar you want to remove.

> **NOTE** *If you turn on Excel's personalized menus and toolbars, that setting also affects how toolbars appear. Refer to the Personalized Menus and Toolbars entry for more information.*

Customizing a Toolbar

To add buttons to a toolbar, follow these steps:

1. Make sure the toolbar is currently visible.
2. Choose the Tools→Customize command and click the Commands tab (see Figure T-5).

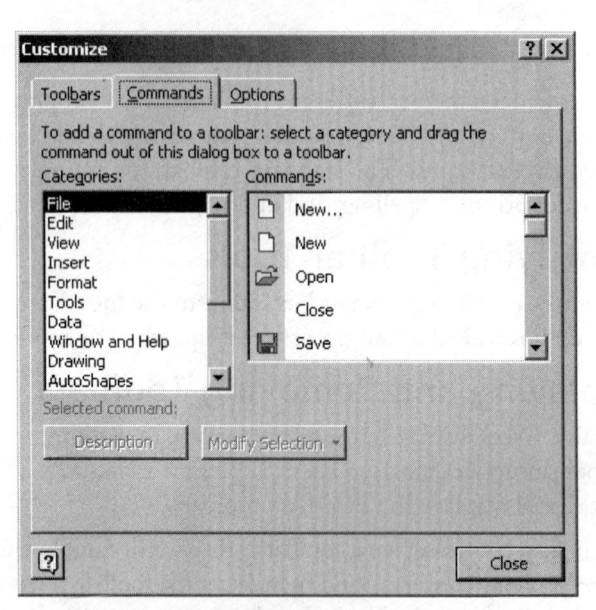

Figure T-5   The Commands tab of the Customize dialog box.

3. Select the command category from the Categories list box that includes the command you want to add to a toolbar.

4. Scroll through the Commands list box. When you see the command you want to add to the toolbar, drag it to the toolbar.

> NOTE   *You can also customize a toolbar by clicking on the arrow button at the very right end of the toolbar, choosing the Add Or Remove buttons command, and then the name of the toolbar. For example, to customize the Formatting toolbar, click the arrow button and choose Add Or Remove Buttons and then Formatting. Excel displays a complete list of the buttons commonly placed on the toolbar. To add a button, select it from the list.*

To remove a button from a toolbar, follow these steps:

1. Click on the arrow button at the very right end of the toolbar.

2. Choose the Add Or Remove buttons command, and then the name of the toolbar. For example, to customize the Formatting toolbar, click the arrow button, choose Add Or Remove Buttons and then Formatting.

3. When Excel displays a complete list of the buttons commonly placed on the toolbar, select the button you want to remove. Excel identifies which buttons are already on the toolbar by marking them with a checkmark.

SEE ALSO *Personalized Menus and Toolbars*

Tracing Errors see Formula Auditing

Troubleshooting

You can suffer from two types of trouble when you work with Excel.

The first type of trouble amounts to operational trouble working with the program—often because you're still learning how to use Excel. When you experience this type of trouble—and assuming you can't get your answer from this book—use the Office Assistant to ask a question. If you don't get the answer from the first set of help topics that the Office Assistant suggests, try rephrasing your question using different words.

The second type of trouble stems from mechanical problems with the Excel program itself or perhaps one of the other programs running on your computer. Surprisingly, you often can solve mechanical problems, too, if you visit Microsoft's KnowledgeBase web site. The Microsoft KnowledgeBase web site provides troubleshooting information about solving all sorts of mechanical problems and bugs working with Excel.

To use the Microsoft KnowledgeBase Web site, open your web browser and enter the following URL into the Address box:

http://search.support.microsoft.com/kb/c.asp

When your Web browser opens the KnowledgeBase search form, Select Microsoft Excel from the My Search Is About box, type your question into the My Question Is box, and press Enter (see Figure T-6). The search results page that the KnowledgeBase server displays will display a list of KnowledgeBase articles that provide troubleshooting information that seems to be related the problem you describe.

U   Excel 2002 From A to Z

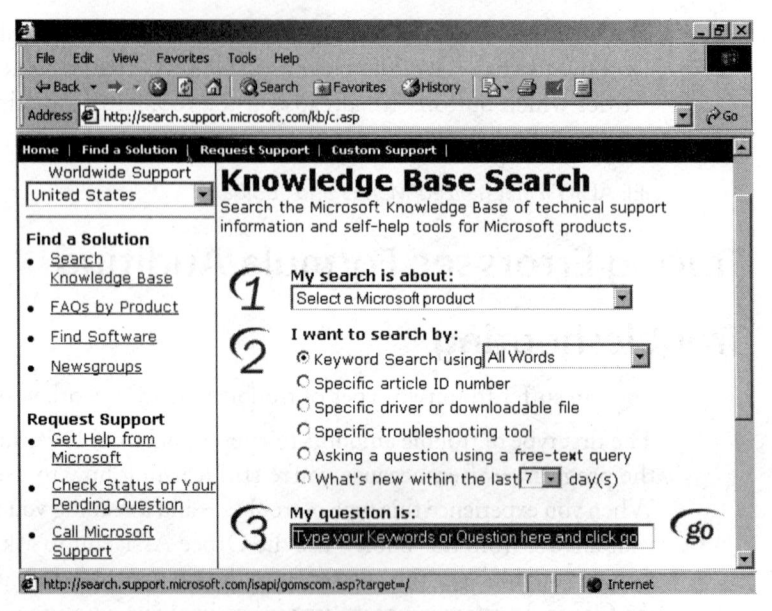

Figure T-6 The KnowledgeBase search form.

Undeleting Workbooks see Workbooks

Underlining

Within Excel, you have two tools for underlining text. Which tool you use depends on the underlining you want.

- To underline the selected text with a single line, click the Underline button on the Formatting toolbar.
- To underline the selected text with a double line or a dashed line, choose the Format→Cells command and select an underlining option from the Underline list box.

Undoing Mistakes

If you make a mistake while entering data or editing your worksheet, you can use the Undo toolbar button to reverse the effects of your last actions. You can also undo the Undo operation by clicking the Redo toolbar button. To reverse the effects of a series of most recent actions, click the arrow beside the Undo toolbar button and select multiple actions from the list. To redo a series of last actions, click the arrow beside the Redo toolbar button and select multiple actions from the list.

URLs

URL is an acronym that stands for Uniform Resource Locator. The Internet uses URLs as Internet addresses. A URL typically includes four components: the protocol, the server, the path, and the file name. For example, in the URL below, *http://* is the protocol, *www.redtechpress.com* is the server, */tocs/* is the path, and *mbaexcel.pdf* is the file.

http://www.redtechpress.com/tocs/mbaexcel.pdf

NOTE   *http:// is one of the protocols used to display Web pages.*

You can use URLs when you save and open files if you have permission to use the Web server. To do this, simply enter the complete URL into the File Name box on the Save As or Open dialog box. The Web server you're referencing will probably ask you for a password.

SEE ALSO *File Extensions, File names, Pathnames*

Values

Values are numbers you want to add, subtract, multiply, divide, or otherwise manipulate in formulas. In a budgeting worksheet, for example, you would enter the budgeted amounts as values (see Figure V-1).

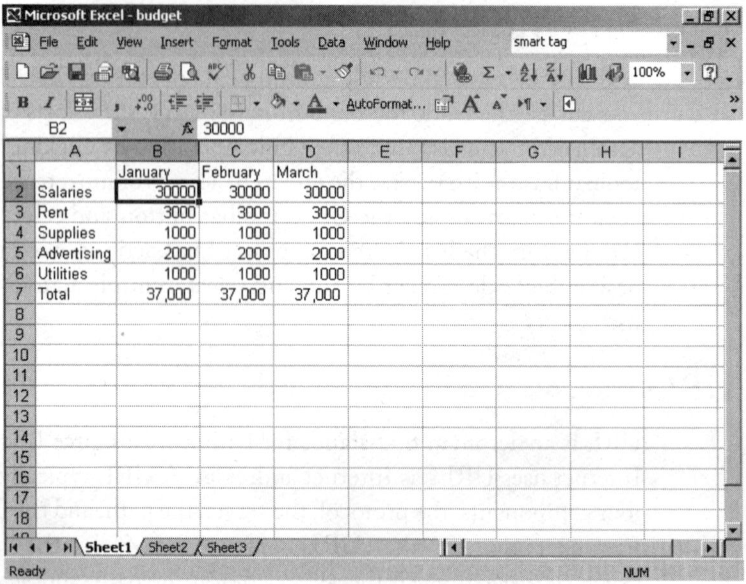

Figure V-1 A budgeting worksheet with labels and values.

To enter values, use the ten number keys either on the main keyboard or on the numeric keypad. To use the numeric keypad, the Num Lock key must be selected. Use the period key to show decimal places and the hyphen key to identify negative values.

To enter values, use the same three-step process as you do to enter labels. For example, to enter the value 3000 shown in cell B2, move the cell selector to the desired cell, type the value, and set the value in the cell—by pressing the Enter key, clicking the Enter button on the formula bar, or moving to another cell.

SEE ALSO *Labels, Scientific Notation*

Views

Excel displays your workbooks either in a Normal View or a Page Break View.

To switch from one view to another, choose the View→Normal View or the View→Page Break View command.

NOTE   The Views→Custom Views command lets you create custom views of a workbook based on printing settings, hidden rows and columns, and first filters.

SEE ALSO *Outlining*

Visual Basic

Microsoft builds a programming language, called Visual Basic for Applications, into the Excel program. When you create a macro, for example, what Excel actually does is write a Visual Basic program to perform the recorded actions.

SEE ALSO *Macros*

Web Components see Web Pages

Web Pages

You can save an Excel workbook as web page. To do so, use the File→Save As command to save the workbook in almost the usual way—except use the Save File As Type box to indicate that you want to save the workbook as a web page (see Figure W-1) and click the Publish button. Excel adds two Save buttons—Entire Workbook and Selection—to let you specify how much of the workbook you want to turn into the web page. Mark the Save button that corresponds to your choice.

TIP   *You can enter a pathname that uses a URL into the Filename box.*

X Excel 2002 From A to Z

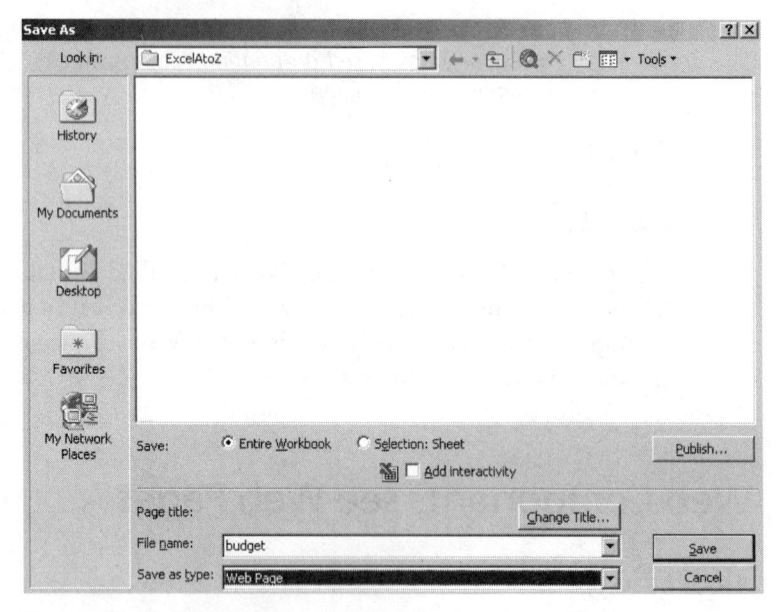

Figure W-1 The Save As dialog box as it appears when you save a workbook as a web page.

Check the Add Interactivity box to tell Excel that it should turn the Excel workbook into a Web page that uses Web spreadsheet components. A Web page that uses Web spreadsheet components lets someone viewing the workbook web page to actually work with the spreadsheet. For example, a Web page browser can change inputs and see formula results updated automatically.

> **NOTE** *In order for a Web spreadsheet component to work, the user needs to possess the appropriate Microsoft Office license.*

What-if Tables see Data Tables

Window Panes

Excel lets you split the workbook window into panes so you can see different portions of a workbook in different panes. To split the workbook window into panes, move the cell selector to the cell where you want the split and choose the Window→Split command. To later unsplit the window, choose the Window→Remove Split command.

Excel 2002 From A to Z

TIP *To freeze a pane so that it scrolls whenever you scroll the workbook's other panes, choose the Window@—>Freeze command. To unfreeze a pane so it doesn't scroll, choose the Window→Unfreeze command.*

WordArt

You can turn text into a graphics object. To do this, you use the WordArt applet. WordArt, like Microsoft Graph, is a small miniprogram, or applet, that comes with Office programs including Microsoft Excel.

Creating a WordArt Object

To create a piece of text using WordArt, choose the Insert→Picture→WordArt command. When you do, Excel starts the WordArt program. The first window you'll see is the WordArt Gallery (see Figure W-2).

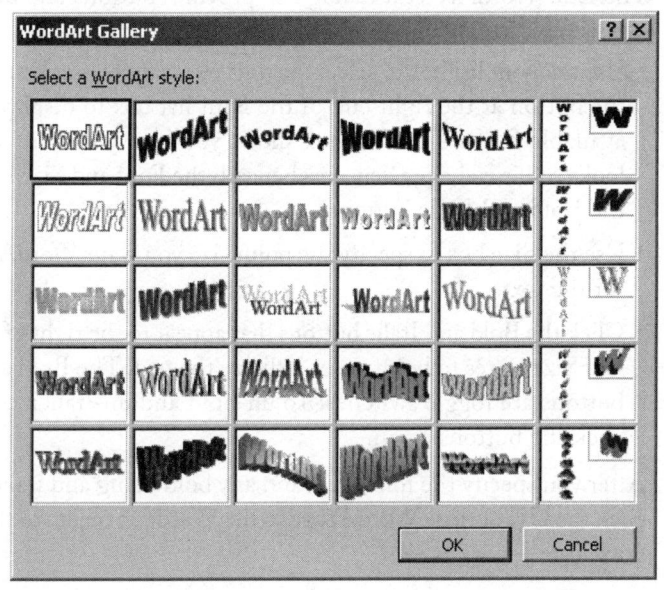

Figure W-2   The WordArt Gallery window.

This window shows you the various ways you can display the selected text as a graphics image. You select a Word Art Style, click OK, and then type your text into the next dialog box that Word Art displays (see Figure W-3).

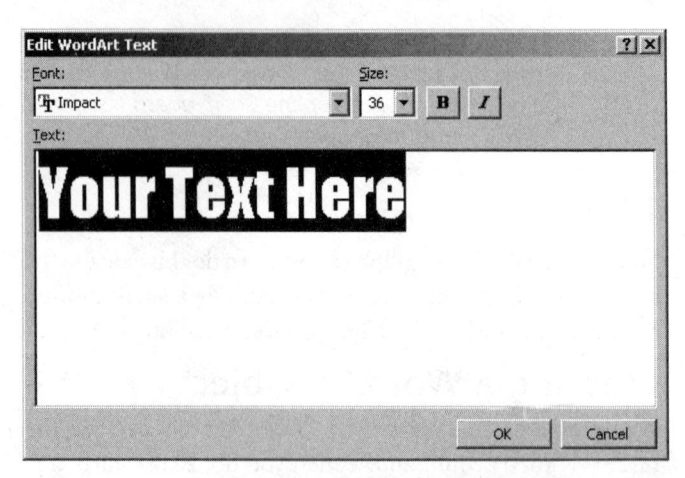

Figure W-3 The Edit WordArt Text dialog box.

The Edit WordArt Text dialog box provides buttons and boxes you can use to format your WordArt object:

- Use the Font list box to select the font you want to use. You can click the button at the right end of the Font list box to display a list of available fonts. The Text box shows you how your font selection looks—this is the preview area beneath the Font and Size boxes and the Bold and Italic buttons.

- Use the Size box to specify the point size you want WordArt to use for the text.

- Click the Bold and Italic buttons that appear to the right of the Font and Size boxes to boldface or italicize the text. The Bold and Italic buttons are toggle switches: To un-bold and un-italicize the text, click the buttons again.

After you specify the font, size, and any boldfacing and italicization, click the OK button. WordArt adds the WordArt object to the workbook (see Figure W-4).

Excel 2002 From A to Z

W

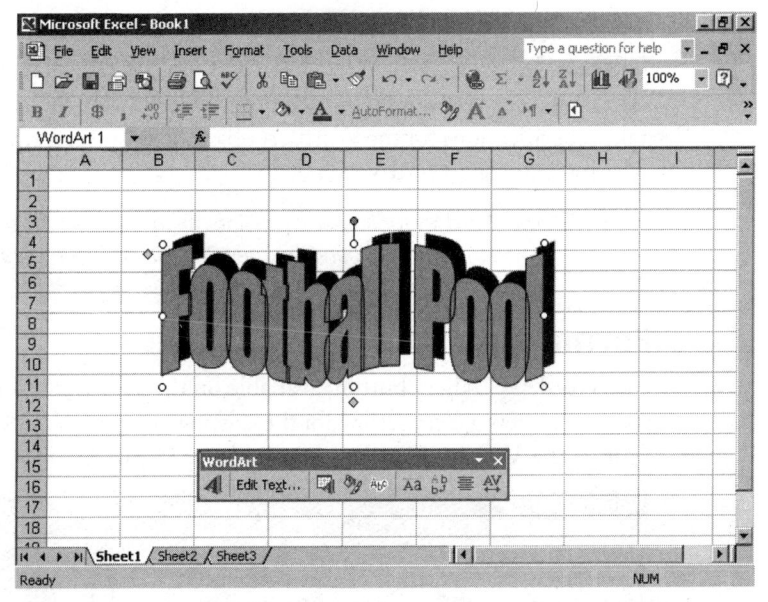

Figure W-4   A WordArt object.

NOTE   *You can double-click the new WordArt image to redisplay the Edit WordArt window.*

Moving and Resizing WordArt Objects

After WordArt adds the object to the workbook, you can move and resize the object by clicking and dragging. To correctly position the WordArt object, drag it to the appropriate location. To resize the object, drag the selection handles that surround the object. To change the WordArt effect, you can also typically drag the yellow diamond marker. You would drag this marker, for example, to make a leaning WordArt object lean more or lean less.

Editing WordArt Text

The Edit Text tool, available on WordArt toolbar, redisplays the Edit WordArt Text window so you change the font, size, boldface, and italics specifications for the WordArt object or so you can edit the text used to create the WordArt object.

> **NOTE** *The WordArt toolbar also provides an Insert WordArt tool which you can use to add another new WordArt object to your workbook.*

Formatting WordArt Objects

The WordArt Gallery button, available on the WordArt toolbar, lets you select a new gallery setting for the existing, selected WordArt object using a the WordArt Gallery window (see Figure W-5).

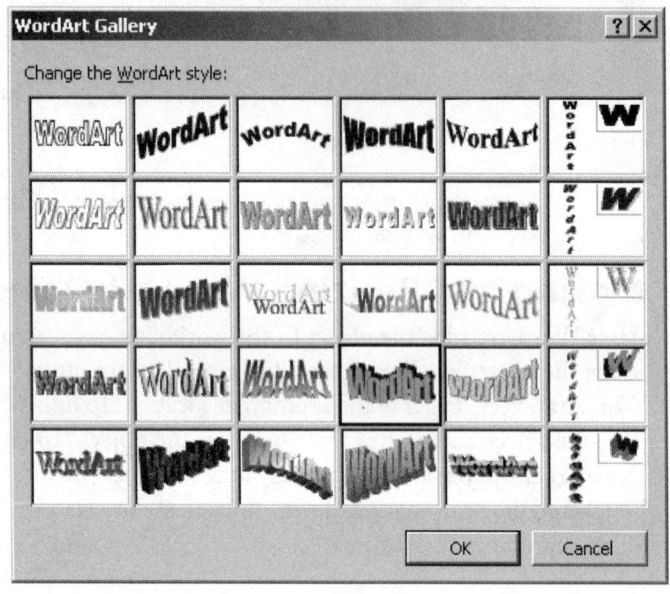

Figure W-5 The WordArt Gallery window.

> **NOTE** *To remove the WordArt toolbar, simply click the workbook, Excel removes the WordArt toolbar. If you later want to make additional changes to the WordArt object, simply click the WordArt object again. Excel reopens the WordArt toolbar and you can use its buttons to make whatever changes you want.*

The Format WordArt button on the WordArt toolbar lets you change the color used for the WordArt object; the line, color, and style used to draw the WordArt object; and the size and layout of the WordArt object. When you choose the Format WordArt button, WordArt displays the Format WordArt dialog box (see Figure W-6). You can use the Format WordArt dialog box's Colors and Lines tab, for example, to change, predictably, the color and lines used to create the WordArt object. (To make changes, simply use the tab's drop-down list boxes to select different colors, line styles, and so on.)

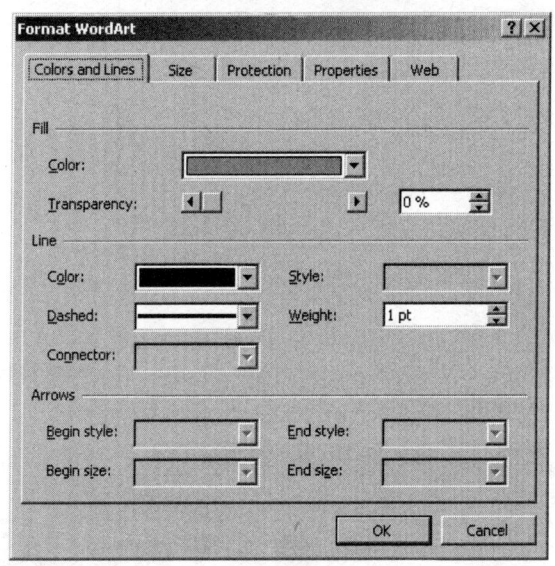

Figure W-6   The Colors And Lines tab of the Format WordArt dialog box.

You can use the Format WordArt dialog box's Size tab to change the dimensions of the WordArt object (see Figure W-7). The other tabs in the Format WordArt dialog box work in a similar fashion.

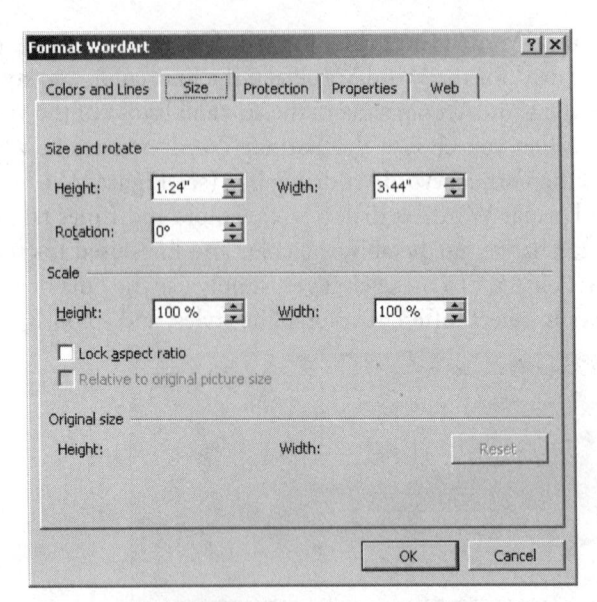

Figure W-7 The Size tab of the Format WordArt dialog box.

The WordArt Shape button displays a menu of pictures you can choose from to select the shape of the WordArt object (see Figure W-8). You simply click the shape you want the WordArt object to take.

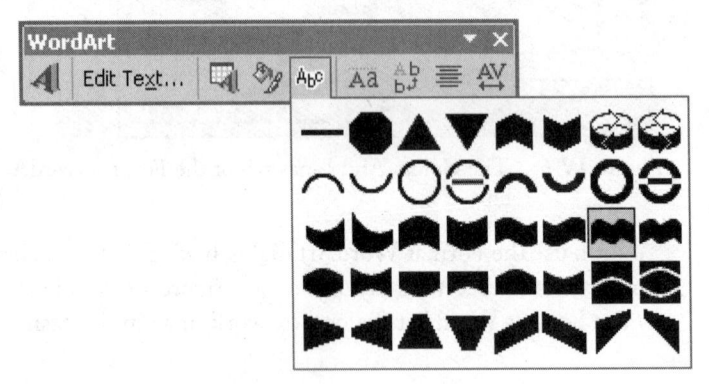

Figure W-8 The WordArt Shape menu.

The Free Rotate button, if clicked, adds selection handles to the WordArt object. You can use these Rotate selection handles to rotate, or spin, the WordArt object on the page.

Excel 2002 From A to Z

The WordArt Same Letter Heights tool lets you tell WordArt that each letter in the WordArt graphics image should be the same height. The WordArt Same Letter Heights button is a toggle switch. If you click it again, WordArt resizes the letter heights back to their original sizes.

The WordArt Vertical Text toolbar lets you flip the WordArt text so that it's vertical rather than horizontal. WordArt also adds selection handles after you click the tool. You can use these selection handles to rotate the object.

The WordArt Alignment button displays a menu of text-alignment options (see Figure W-9). You simply select the menu command that refers to the text alignment you want to use for text in the WordArt object.

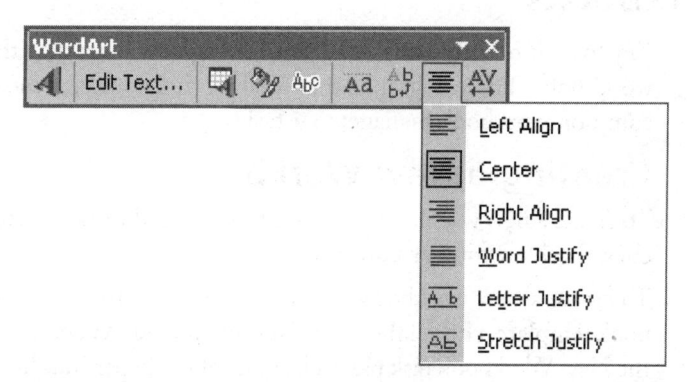

Figure W-9   The WordArt Alignment menu.

The WordArt Character Spacing tool, the last one on the toolbar displays a menu of character-spacing commands (see Figure W-10). You choose the character-spacing command that refers to the type of spacing you want for the text that makes the WordArt object.

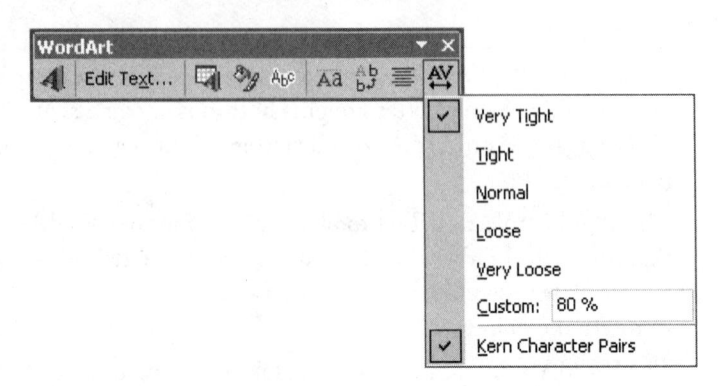

Figure W-10 The WordArt Character Spacing menu

Workbooks

Key to comfortably using Excel is knowing how to work with Excel's workbooks. The paragraphs that follow briefly describe most of the common workbook management tasks.

Creating a New Workbook

To create a new workbook that uses the standard workbook template, click the New toolbar button.

To create a new workbook based on other than the standard workbook template, choose the File→New command. When Excel opens the New Workbook task pane, click one of the hyperlinks listed in the New or New From Template areas (see Figure W-11).

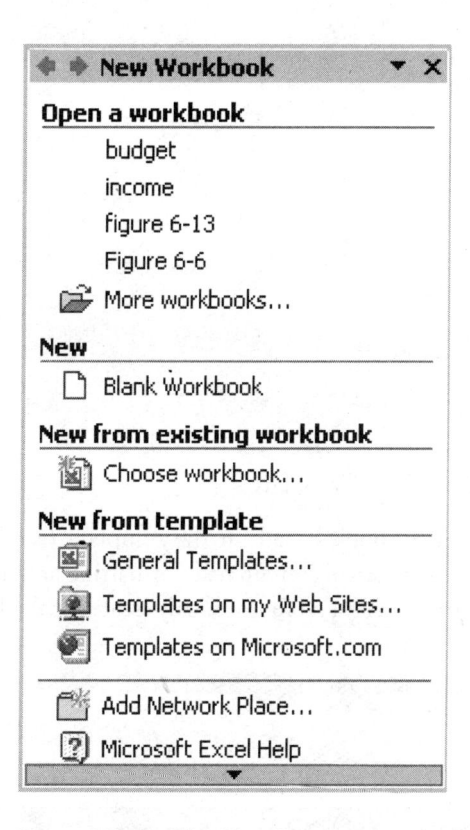

Figure W-11 The New Workbook task pane.

If you click the General Templates hyperlink, Excel displays the Templates dialog box (see Figure W-12). Click the tab that seems to most closely match the category of workbook you want. Then, double-click the template icon that most closely matches the specific workbook you want.

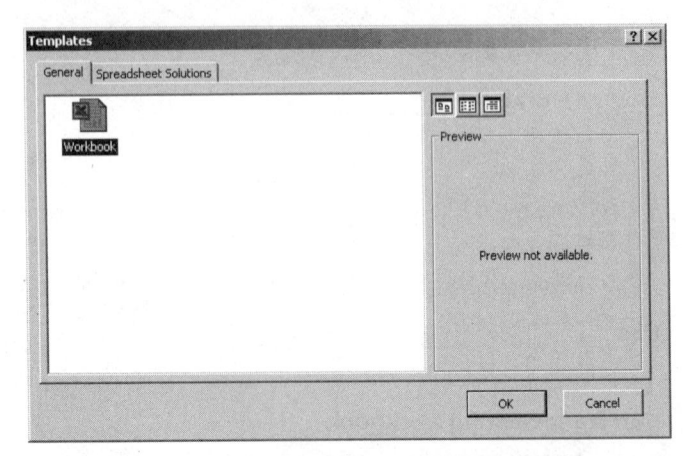

Figure W-12 The Templates dialog box.

Excel opens a new workbook based on the template (see Figure W-13). This new workbook will contain text, formatting and instructions you can use to more easily and more quickly create the final workbook.

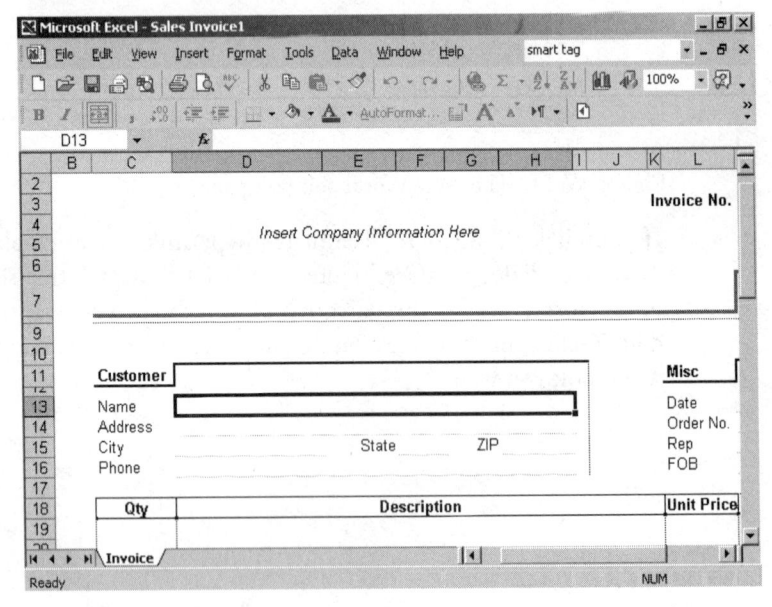

Figure W-13 A workbook created from the Sales Invoice template.

NOTE   *The Templates On My Web Sites and Templates On Microsoft.com hyperlinks, also available in the New Workbook pane, let you retrieve Excel templates over the Internet and Web.*

Opening a Workbook

You have several convenient choices for opening documents in Excel.

- **Documents menu.** If a workbook is listed under the Documents menu (displayed when you click the Start button and point to the Documents command) you can open the workbook by clicking it on the Documents menu.

- **New Workbook pane.** When you start Excel, the New Workbook task pane lists workbooks you've recently used and provides hyperlinks you can click to create a new workbook.

- **File menu list.** If a workbook is one you've recently opened using Excel, the workbook may be listed at the bottom of the File menu. In this case, you can open the workbook by choosing it from the File menu.

- **File→Open command.** You can choose the File→Open command to display the Open dialog box (see Figure W-14). To use the Open dialog box, first select the folder containing your workbook from the Look In list box. Then, when Excel lists the documents in that folder, scroll through the list until you find the one you're looking for. When you see it, double-click it to open it.

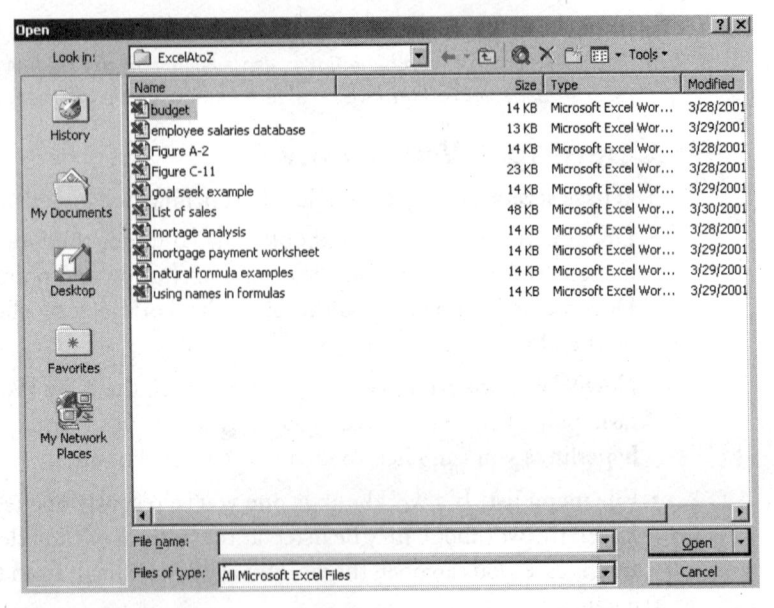

Figure W-14 The Open dialog box.

- **Open toolbar button.** You can also click the Open toolbar button to display the Open dialog box (see Figure W-14). Again, to use the Open dialog box, select the folder containing your workbook from the Look In list box, scroll through the list of documents until you find the one you're looking for, and then double-click that workbook to open it.

- **My Computer or Windows Explorer.** If you use the My Computer window or Windows Explorer to display the folder containing your workbook, you can double-click the workbook to open it (see Figure W-15). When you open an Excel workbook, Windows first starts Excel and then instructs Excel to open the workbook.

Excel 2002 From A to Z

W

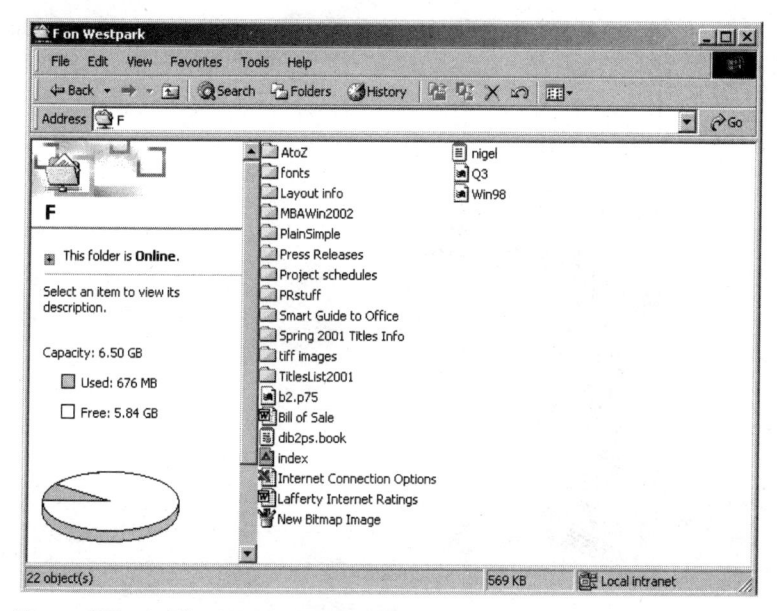

Figure W-15 The My Computer Window.

Closing a Workbook

To close a workbook, choose the File→Close command or click the workbook window's Close box.

NOTE   *If you've made changes to a workbook that haven't been saved, Excel asks if you want to save your workbook or lose your changes.*

TIP   *You can close all the open workbooks by holding down the Shift key and then choosing the File→Close All command.*

Saving a Workbook

To save a workbook, choose the File→Save command or click the Save toolbar button.

The first time you choose the File→Save command or click the Save toolbar button for new workbook, Excel displays the Save As dialog box so you can name the file and specify where it should be saved (see Figure W-16). To use the Save As dialog box, follow these steps:

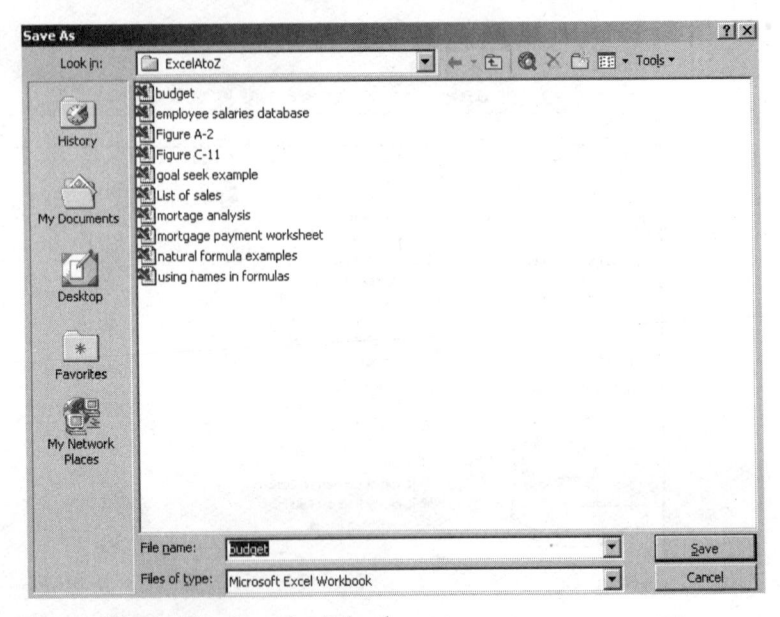

Figure W-16 The Save As dialog box.

1. Use the Save In box to pick the folder you want to save the workbook in.
2. Enter the name you want to use for the workbook into the File Name box.
3. (Optional) If you want to use this workbook with other programs or share the workbook with someone who doesn't have Excel, open the Save As Type list box and select a file format.

> NOTE *Excel's workbook file format is readable by many other programs, but if you want to be sure that a workbook can be read by almost any program select the Text (Tab Delimited) file type.*

Re-saving a Workbook

The subsequent times you save a workbook—the times after you've provided a name and specified a folder location—you also save the workbook using the File→Save command or the Save toolbar button. When you re-save a workbook, however, Excel doesn't display the Save dialog box. It assumes you want to use the same file name and location.

Excel 2002 From A to Z

W

Renaming and Relocating a Workbook

To name a workbook or relocate a workbook you've already saved, choose the File→Save As command. When Excel displays the Save As dialog box, rename or relocate the workbook.

Deleting a Workbook

To delete a workbook, use the My Computer window or the Windows Explorer to display the folder holding the workbook. Then right-click the workbook and choose the Delete command (see Figure W-17).

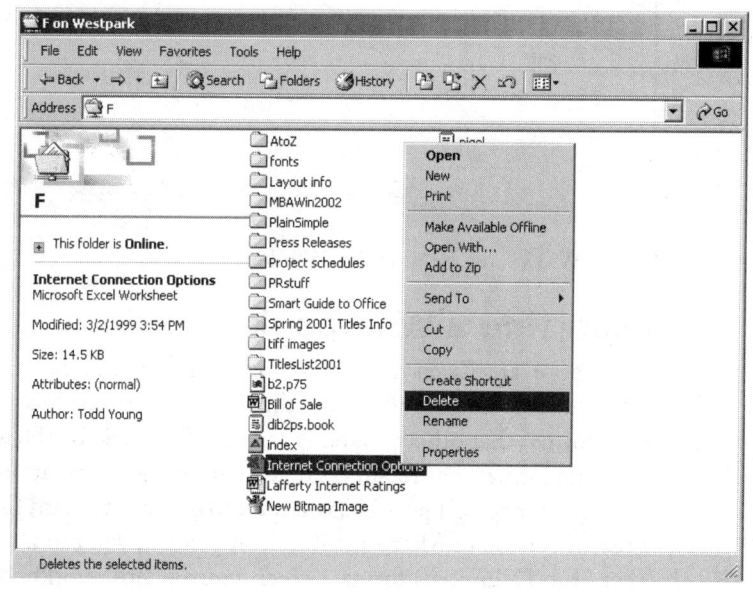

Figure W-17 The My Computer window showing the Shortcut menu.

Undeleting a Workbook

You may be able to undelete, or restore, a workbook you've previously deleted. Windows sets aside a percentage of your hard disk space to store recently deleted files. To see which deleted files Windows is still storing, double-click the Recycle Bin icon, which appears on the Windows Desktop. Windows opens the Recycle Bin window, which lists all the recently deleted files (see Figure W-18). Scroll through the list. If you can find your workbook, right-click it and choose Restore from the shortcut menu.

187

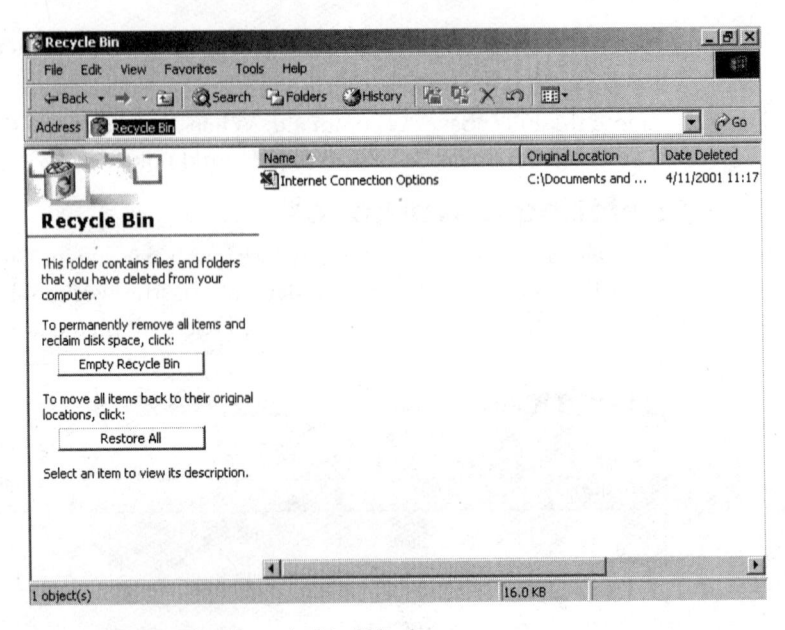

Figure W-18 The Recycle Bin Window.

Exporting a Workbook

To export an Excel workbook, save the workbook using the File→Save As command but use the Save As Type list box to choose a file format that other programs can use. The trick, by the way, is to use a file format that retains as much workbook information as possible. That means, if possible, you want to use the standard format for a recent version of Microsoft Excel. In a pinch, you can also use the Text (Tab Delimited) format, which returns most workbook information including labels, values, and formulas. In a worst case situation, you can use the plain text format, which lets you export the text of your workbook but not anything else.

Importing a Workbook

To import a workbook into Excel—say a workbook someone created using another spreadsheet program—just open the workbook. Excel comes with a large set of filters that let it open most popular spreadsheet documents.

Printing a Workbook

To print a workbook, click the Print toolbar button or choose the File→Print command. If you click the Print button, Excel prints your workbook using the default, or usual, print settings. If you choose the Print command, Excel displays the Print dialog box (see Figure W-19).

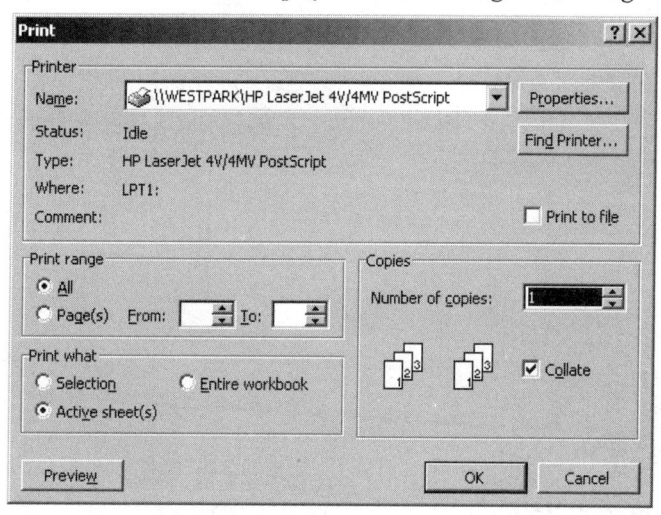

Figure W-19 The Print dialog box.

Use the Print dialog box's buttons and boxes to specify exactly how Excel should print:

- Choose the printer you want to print the workbook from the Name list box, if the Name box doesn't already show the printer.

- Use the Print Range buttons to indicate whether you want to print all the pages in the workbook, just the current page, or some set of pages.

- Use the Copies boxes to specify the number of copies you want printed and whether copies should be collated.

- Use the Print What list box to indicate whether you want to print the current selection, the active worksheet or the entire workbook, the workbook.

Previewing a Workbook

You can preview what your printed workbook will look like by choosing the File→Print Preview command (see Figure W-20).

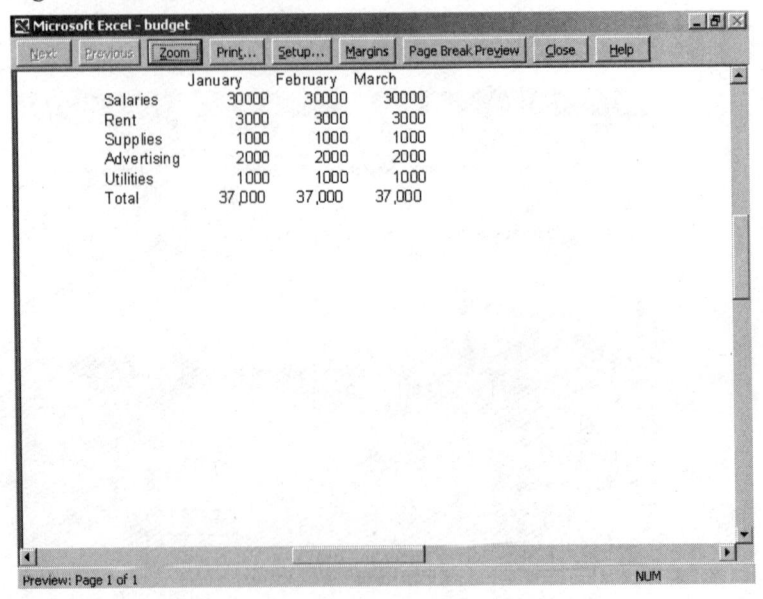

Figure W-20 The Print Preview window.

The Print Preview window includes a toolbar with several handy tools for previewing your workbook:

- **Print button.** When you want to print the workbook, click the Print button. Or, choose the File→Print command.
- **Zoom.** The Zoom button is a toggle switch that tells Excel when you click the workbook, Excel should alternatively magnify or reduce the size of the preview display.
- **Next.** The Next button displays the next page of the to-be-printed workbook.
- **Previous.** The Previous button displays the previous page of the to-be-printed workbook.

- **Setup.** The Setup button displays the Page Setup dialog box so you can adjust the page orientation, margins, header or footer and sheet printing settings.
- **Margins.** The Margins button adds movable margins lines to the print preview window. To move, or change, the margins, drag the margin lines.
- **Page Break Preview/ Normal View.** The Page Break Preview/Normal view button together between a normal workbook view and page break preview view of the workbook and returns you to the regular Excel program window.
- **Close.** The Close button closes the Print Preview button and returns you to the regular Excel program window.
- **Help.** The Help button lets you click some item, such as a button or menu command, and see relevant information from the Excel help information file.

Dividing Workbooks

You can split a workbook that's grown too large by cutting portions out of the workbook and pasting them into other new documents. Refer to the entry on Moving Text for information about how to do this.

Worksheets

A worksheet provides columns and rows you use to enter labels, values, and formulas (see Figure W-21). Excel workbooks always include worksheets. They may also include chart sheets and macro sheets.

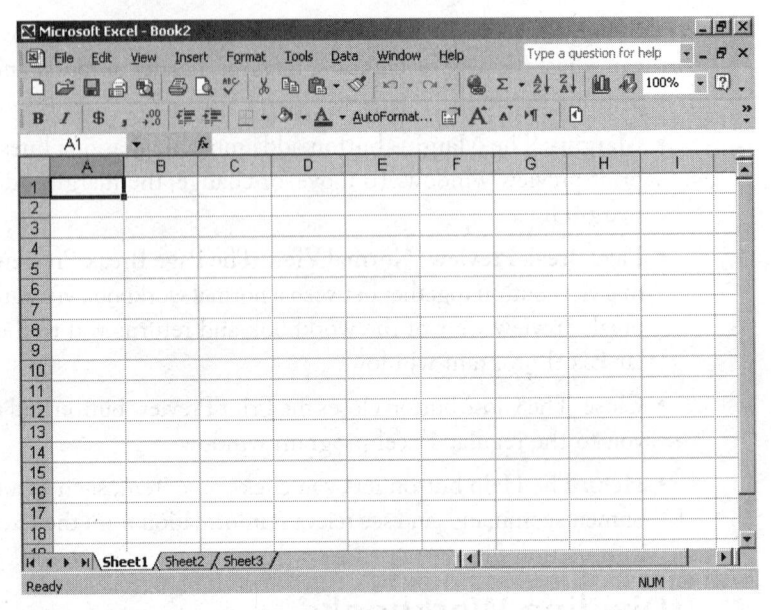

Figure W-21 An Excel workbook showing an empty worksheet.

To add a new worksheet to the workbook, choose the Insert→Worksheet command.

SEE ALSO *Charts, Macros, Sheets*

XML

XML, an acronym for Extensible Markup Language, stores information in files that use standard formats so the files can be read by other programs. Excel can read many XML files and even has its own XML spreadsheet format.

SEE ALSO *HTML*

XY Charts see Charts

Zoom

The Zoom box, which often appears on the Standard toolbar, lets you magnify or reduce the size of the workbook that shows in the workbook window to some percentage of its actual size (see Figure W-22). To use the Zoom box, enter a percent in the Zoom box or open the Zoom list box by clicking its arrow and select a zoom percentage from the list.

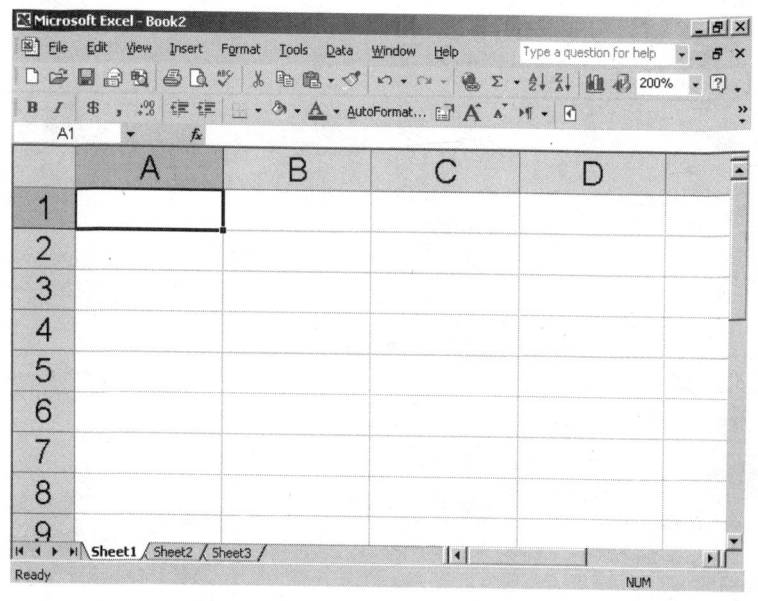

Figure W-22 An Excel workbook "zoomed" to 200% of its original size.

40   E R E   O   N E
A₁ B₁ C D₀ E₁ F₁ A₂ G₁ F₅ H₁ I₁ A₃ J₁ D₄ K₁

         E   R   E O
43 A₄ L₁ D₂ I₂ E₂ M₁ N₁ D₃ H₂

                        E   O   V E
44¹ O₁ P₁ Q F₂ D₄ I H₃ M₂ D₅

   N   V   P
44² J₂ D₆ M₃ D₇ E₃

      E   V   E   R Y
46¹ D₈ I₃ H₄ M₄ F₃ R₁ E₄ D₉ R₂ A₅ E₅ F₄

            E E
46² L₂ Q₂ D₁₀ D₁₁ T₁ L₃ C₂ N₂ Q₃
       S₁   S₂